Unexpected Israel

Unexpected Israel

Stories You Never Read in the Media

Ruth Corman

gefen
publishing house
JERUSALEM ◆ NEW YORK
Est. 1981

Images for the "Joseph Bau House" article are courtesy of the Joseph Bau House Museum, www.josephbau.com, 9 Berdichevsky St., Tel Aviv

Cover design: Leah Ben Avraham/Noonim Graphics
Typesetting: Renana Typesetting

ISBN: 978-965-229-851-5

1 3 5 7 9 8 6 4 2

Gefen Publishing House Ltd.

6 Hatzvi Street
Jerusalem 94386, Israel
972-2-538-0247
orders@gefenpublishing.com

Gefen Books

11 Edison Place
Springfield, NJ 07081
516-593-1234
orders@gefenpublishing.com

www.gefenpublishing.com

Printed in Israel

Send for our free catalog

LIBRARY OF CONGRESS CATALOGING-IN-PUBLICATION DATA

Corman, Ruth, author.
  Unexpected Israel : quirky and moving stories you never read in the media / by Ruth Corman.
    pages cm
  ISBN 978-965-229-851-5
  1. Israel. I. Title.
  DS126.5.C65 2015
  956.94--dc23

2015030826

Contents

Preface

In 2008 I wrote the life story of David Rubinger, the acclaimed Israeli photo journalist. It took three years to complete and is probably one of the first books ever to be written on Skype. But despite excellent sales and its publication in three languages, I never considered myself a writer.

When I started an extensive book tour of the United States, the immigration official at Newark asked me the purpose of my visit – was it business or pleasure? I hesitated. "A bit of each, I guess. I'm promoting a book." "Are you a writer?" he asked. "I don't think so," I replied. "Listen, Ma'am," he said patiently, "have you written a book or not?" "Well, yes," I responded, to which he retorted, "Well, sure as hell you're an author, Ma'am – just go for it, girl!" And so I entered the New World in my capacity as a wordsmith.

From this unexpected beginning, I developed a passion for research and for putting words onto paper and I knew that this was what I wanted to do.

The inspiration for *Unexpected Israel* followed the discovery of *India Exposed* by Clive Limpkin (Abbeville Press, 2009). *India Exposed* comprised short, pithy and amusing texts, accompanied by Clive's brilliant photography. He focused on everyday, iconic or unusual things that caught his eye during his travels in India.

Reading his book sowed the seeds of an idea for me to produce something similar, but in this case focusing on Israel. It was already evident to me by the way Israel was portrayed in the British press that there was a great lack of understanding about the country and the only items covered focused on conflict.

I decided to try to show a side of Israel that rarely receives attention – the creative, amusing, quirky and moving aspects of the country. I began the book over four years ago and to date there are more than one hundred stories, each with my accompanying photographs.

Alon Galili has been my guide and inspiration. I was fortunate in the early days to meet him and he has become my guide, friend and source of all knowledge about Israel. He is a gifted storyteller – a man of the people, loved by everyone who meets him for his warmth, generosity, kindness and encyclopedic knowledge in many fields.

I asked him to show me the lesser-known places in Israel, a challenge he enthusiastically welcomed. Together we took long, bumpy rides off piste in his 4×4, from the northern border with Lebanon down to Eilat in the south. Alon has the capacity to bring everything to life – even in the most arid landscape. Through him I have been introduced to many of the people and places that feature in this book.

John Harlow was a friend I met through my art consultancy in 2013. We spoke on the telephone nearly every day but never actually met. He had established a worldwide media corporation, then sold it and retired, at age forty-four, to a beach house near Brighton to relax and decide what to do next. He was creative, talented, witty and gentle; he composed music, wrote and painted. We exchanged many emails and he read my stories.

John wanted to work with me and suggested that I regard him as the target market for my book. He explained: "I am university educated, widely traveled and known as an innovative mover in the international world of marketing. In spite of this I am shocked to realize that I know nothing about

Israel." He continued: "Your stories have opened my eyes – you must publish them."

By this time I had written many of the stories but was struggling to find a title. I asked John for help and a couple of days later he came up with the perfect title, Unexpected Israel. But, tragically he died two weeks later, just after his forty-fifth birthday, in August 2013. I owe a lot to this special friend, who put himself out to help me and encouraged me to persevere. I am just sad that he is not here to see the project reach fruition.

Steve Linde, the editor in chief of the *Jerusalem Post*, then offered me a monthly column where my tales are featured. At about the same time I set up an internet blogsite where the stories could be read. Since then its readership has gone up to almost ten thousand, from nearly sixty countries.

During this time I have received hundreds of emails from readers all over the world. One surprise was the reaction from Israelis. I had not initially considered them as my audience, assuming that they knew everything about their own country – but this has proved to be quite the reverse. I delight in receiving their letters thanking me for introducing them to aspects of Israel about which they were unaware.

Charles Corman has the double role of being not only my husband but my brilliant editor. I give him drafts – feeling like a schoolgirl handing in homework, and they are returned with infinitives un-split as well as other more helpful suggestions. I always expect to see "4/10 for effort – must try harder!" written across the bottom of the page. I am constantly amazed at how he can find things to improve after I have re-edited the text at least twenty times – no doubt it is his years as a lawyer.

Dorothy Bohm, the doyenne of British photography, has been my photographic mentor for many years. She has been an unfailing source of advice and encouragement without which I doubt I would ever have considered showing my work in public.

Victor Daniels, my late father, is the person to whom I dedicated this book even before I started to write it. When he died he left me with an amazing legacy – the gift of curiosity. I remember, when man first landed on the moon, that he said how annoyed he would be to die because he might miss something exciting happening after he had gone. How he would have enjoyed this voyage of discovery that I embarked upon. He was interested in just about everything and in a strange way I feel that, through my writing, I am becoming more and more like him, so thanks a lot, Dad.

Finally thanks to **Ilan Greenfield** and his team at Gefen Publishing. It has been a pleasure to work with you.

She lived in a primitive mud hut, walking everywhere barefoot.

Tsegue-Mariam

Addis Ababa to Jerusalem: A Musical Legend

I first heard of Tsegue-Mariam from my nephew in California, who asked if I knew about an Ethiopian nun living in Israel. I was intrigued. Something of a cult figure in music circles, she had been sequestered for the past thirty years in the Ethiopian convent in Jerusalem.

Her story reads like a movie script, and the more I researched the more dramatic it became. Born in 1923 into an aristocratic family with close connections to Emperor Haile Selassie, she and her sister were the first Ethiopian girls ever sent to school in Switzerland. She was six years old. Everything was new and strange – the language, the weather, the food and the people.

It was there she heard her first piano concerto –

a profound experience that altered her life. She began studying violin and taught herself piano, demonstrating a rare talent. Five years later, she returned home, but shortly afterwards her entire family were taken prisoners of war by Mussolini's invading Italian army and exiled for almost four years. On her eventual return to Addis Ababa, there was little classical music tuition available but she was thrilled to receive an invitation to study in London, an offer dependent on approval from the Ethiopian authorities. To her dismay they refused.

Tsegue-Mariam fell into a deep depression, refusing food, until, close to death and hospitalized, she requested holy communion. Four priests came to her and performed the ceremony.

This was the second major turning point in her life. She embraced religion with a passion, was ordained as a nun and entered a convent where, for ten years, she lived in a primitive mud hut, walking everywhere barefoot.

The death of the bishop in the area where the convent was located prompted a return to Addis Ababa, where her musical career blossomed. She produced several albums, vowing to use her talent to help disadvantaged children through a foundation set up for this purpose by her niece. This led to a great deal of media attention as word spread about her singular contribution to the world of music.

In the late sixties she and her mother visited Jerusalem. She loved the city and, as she spoke German, English, French and Italian fluently, was able to work as a translator for the Ethiopian patriarch. Tsegue-Mariam eventually returned to Addis Ababa but, on the death of her mother in 1984, fled back to Jerusalem to escape the anti-religious Marxist government then in power in Ethiopia. She has remained there ever since.

In 2011 Maya Dunietz, an Israeli musician who had met Tsegue-Mariam briefly six years earlier, received a phone call from her: "I need your help. I am getting old and want my music to be published. She handed over crumpled Air Ethiopia bags crammed with her handwritten pages. Maya spent two years diligently translating Tsegue-Mariam's unique musical language into conventional notation until eventually, in 2013, it was published in time for her ninetieth birthday.

To coincide with this, her life story was beautifully written by Meytal Ofer. Meytal told me: "As Tsegue-Mariam had never left the convent for sixteen years I invited her to visit my family, who live by the sea. It was a privilege to share her joy on seeing the ocean after so long and her delight in the simple pleasure of eating an ice cream."

The Jerusalem Sacred Music Festival organized a celebration concert, where for the first

She handed
over crumpled
Air Ethiopia
bags crammed
with her
handwritten
pages.

time Tsegue-Mariam heard her work performed in public by others. Birthday tributes poured in from all over the world for this diminutive figure who has enriched the lives of so many.

Having extensively researched this story I could not finish it without at least attempting to meet her. I was concerned about how to do this, as I understood she received few visitors and was reluctant to intrude on her privacy. However, in December 2014 I made my way to the Kidane Meheret Church, a rotunda of traditional Ethiopian design surrounded by a small courtyard, located, appropriately, on Ethiopia Street, near Jaffa Road in Jerusalem.

On entering the compound I immediately found myself in another world, far from the downtown hustle and bustle. Men and women, mostly wearing long robes, sat or stood facing the church, where a service was taking place. Some were in deep contemplation, others praying. There was a tangible atmosphere of calm and spirituality.

When I mentioned to a nun of my interest in Tsegue-Mariam she said, "Why don't you speak to her, that is her room over there," pointing to a doorway just feet away from where we stood. I could not refuse such an invitation. Crossing a courtyard with doors set around the perimeter, I entered a tiny cell where this legendary composer sat quietly in a wheelchair, surrounded by her belongings – including, of course, a piano. She looked up as I entered, her welcoming smile illuminating the room.

It is difficult to express my feelings at finally coming face-to-face with someone about whom I knew so much but had never actually met. I felt like a teenage fan meeting her favorite movie star! We began to talk. She speaks perfect English and is as mentally alert as a nineteen year old. She asked if I liked music, and when I replied that I was studying singing her face lit up. "You must come and sing for me," she said. I returned two days later with my music and somewhat hesitatingly embarked upon an aria by Dvorak.

I explained how much I loved singing but that I did not particularly feel the need to perform. At this she gently reprimanded me, saying that what I possessed was a wonderful gift from God, which carried an obligation to be shared with others. She then said that she had written some vocal pieces, and suggested that I choose one to perform (hopefully in English or Hebrew rather than Amharic!)

We spoke of many things. She told me a lot about her early life and that not a day passed without her creating new compositions, most of which, she said, remained in her head until such time as she could commit them to paper.

Her music is unlike anything I have heard before. Maya Dunietz said: "She has a magical touch on the piano, creating her own musical language, classical but not grand. It is intimate, natural, honest and feminine, delicate but profound. Her compositions vividly reflect her life, telling stories of time and place." But the unique sounds she creates can be heard as a fusion of classical, traditional Ethiopian holy and secular themes with, surprisingly, echoes of blues.

Incidentally, one thing I never expected was her extensive knowledge of hi-tech. She suggested I "cut a disc" of my singing for her – this to someone who still thinks of a "gramophone" as the medium for all things musical. She also advised me how to contact her by cellphone from abroad, using the latest free technology.

Meeting Tsegue-Mariam was a rare privilege. She fervently believes it is the hand of God that provides her with the ability, strength and dedication to achieve all that she has done.

Meytal Ofer, her biographer, told me: "She is one of the most extraordinary people I have ever met, spending hours in solitude working on her compositions. The disparity between the sparseness of her room and her spiritual richness reaches deep into my soul."

I could not agree more.

Smoke from
barbecues
blots out the
landscape
and the sun.

Al Ha'esh
(Barbecues)

The man of the house displays his skills

Once a year on Yom Ha'atzmaut, Israel's Independence Day, the entire country celebrates. Official commemorative events focus on the country's achievements, but by far the preferred way of spending the day is *al ha'esh* – a barbecue with family and friends.

From 5:00 A.M., enthusiasts venture forth to establish their claim on the best plot of open ground, grass or parkland – reminiscent of the way in which certain European nationals would rush out to the hotel swimming pool and deposit their towels on deck chairs, thus declaring their territorial rights for the day. In Israel the massive traffic build up causes some revelers to stake their claim on lay-bys (rest stops) and they have even

been seen camping out on the central reservation (median strip) of the highway.

Israel is literally wall-to-wall fires from north to south. The air is thick with the aroma of seared meat combined with that of *neft* (fuel). Smoke blots out the landscape and the sun.

This is the day when the male assumes the role of cook and reigns supreme. His reputation stands or falls on the quality and particularly the quantity of the meat he provides. Connoisseurs of this "national sport" take pride in their range of marinades, spice mixes and jealously guarded family recipes. A normally impatient race, such men have been known to stand calmly fanning the flames for up to forty minutes to achieve a fire that meets their needs.

What most barbeque enthusiasts never learn, however, is how to clean up after their efforts. The day following Yom Ha'atzmaut 2011 a news item reported that 1.5 million visitors came to the national parks and left behind four hundred tons of garbage.

The only shred of comfort is the fact that this amount of rubbish was down by fifty tons on the previous year. At this rate, Israel should have cleaned up totally by 2019.

I personally have never quite understood the fun of eating burnt food. Perhaps this comes from years of living in England, where barbecues represent shivering in a plastic raincoat waiting optimistically for the time to come when one can politely leave and go home.

The passion of Israelis for this form of catering is thought provoking. Perhaps being deprived of the Temple where sacrifices were made, they have embraced barbecues as today's version, providing them with an opportunity to return to this ancient rite.

Family having a picnic

Shopkeepers lie in wait for me, knowing I will happily pay over the odds.

Two brothers in their shop

The Arab Shuk, Jerusalem

The Arab Shuk in Jerusalem is unique – an eclectic mix of biblical imagery and modern-day technology. A boy astride a donkey bobs down a narrow crowded lane much as he might have done in ancient times. Next to him you spy an internet café.

The Old City is divided into four sections, the *shuk* being located in the Christian and Arab quarters. Tourist trinkets abound but one is still seduced by the displays of beads and jewelry, textiles, ceramics, spices and chunks of highly prized frankincense. In between one glimpses touches of everyday life – a barber shop, a coffee house, or someone carrying traditional sweet sage tea from store to store for the owners.

Vendors in the *shuk* have become expert at identifying the country of origin of their customers. They have managed to develop linguistic skills sufficient to converse in a wide range of languages – enough at least to make a sale.

Haggling is expected. "You are the first customer of the day – I give you good price!" "Please come in – only look!" Once you do, you cannot expect to leave for at least half an hour. The haggling process is formalized. As a buyer never show too much enthusiasm. Look disinterested. "How much you want to pay?" they ask. Offer less than half of what you want to give. This will be rejected, whereupon you start to walk away. You are called back, the process continues – sometimes a sale results, sometimes not.

I remember one memorable bargaining episode in China. My husband refused to pay the asking price for a few paltry items. Negotiations began. I waited outside. Twenty-five minutes later he emerged exultant. "How much did you pay?" I asked. He told me. He had ended up paying double the asking price, as he was completely confused by the financial to-ing and fro-ing. But he was happy, as was the storekeeper, and I was happy because it was over.

For my part I loathe bargaining. I cannot do it. This dates back to my childhood when mother would expect to buy everything "wholesale" and I would cringe waiting for her to finish. She told me that there is an eleventh commandment that goes "Thou shalt never pay the retail price." Here is yet another commandment I have broken.

Shopkeepers lie in wait for me – knowing that I will always happily pay over the odds just to get the transaction over and done with.

A treasure trove

The Armenian Experience

Elia in his photographic shop, Old City, Jerusalem

A stroll down a small side street in the Christian Quarter of the Old City of Jerusalem brings you to a treasure-house of photographs by Elia Kahvedjian.

Elia's story is dramatic and powerfully moving. He was only a child when the Armenian Genocide took place in which one and a half million of his countrymen, from a total population of two and a half million, were systematically killed by the Turks – Elia's family alone lost 160 relatives.

The massacre began on April 24, 1915. This "Great Crime" started with the killing of 250 intellectuals and community leaders in Constantinople. The rest of the population were then uprooted and forced to go on a death march hundreds of miles into the desert without food or water.

Five-year-old Elia left Ourfa with his mother and six-month-old sister. For days they trudged and struggled along. People were being killed en route, others died of disease and hunger. Elia recalls seeing mutilated and burning bodies everywhere.

Eventually his mother, realizing she had no strength to continue, left the baby under a tree in the hope that someone would find her and care for her. She had a dreadful premonition that she had reached the place where they would all die. So strong was this feeling that, on seeing a Kurd

Elia's story
demonstrates
the triumph
of hope over
adversity.

passing by, she begged him to take Elia away to safety. That day she was murdered.

Elia went to the Kurd's home, where after being fed and given medicine he was taken to the city of Mardin and sold for two gold coins to an ironsmith. His job was to operate the bellows, but the man beat him regularly, remonstrating. "I paid two gold pieces for you!" The boy never forgot this realization of his "worth" at such a tender age. When the ironmonger's wife died he took another wife who refused to have Elia in their home. He was thrown out and spent the next two years begging for bread.

One day a man approached him, offered him food and took him to a cave. Suddenly Elia slipped and realized that the floor was covered with human bones and skulls. Terrified he ran away. The man, whom it was believed was a cannibal, threw a sword at him, wounding his leg. The psychological and physical scars from that horrific experience remained with him all his life.

Eventually he was rescued by a group of American missionaries who saved more than one hundred thousand children, sending them to orphanages far away from Turkey. He was sent to Nazareth where one of his teachers, a photographer, employed Elia to carry the heavy glass plates necessary for his work. Every day the boy watched, learned and developed a fascination for the art of photography.

At sixteen he had to leave the orphanage to fend for himself. He moved to Jerusalem, lodged in the Armenian Convent in the Old City and found work at a local photographic studio. Over the years his hard work and diligence paid off, until eventually he owned three studios in Jaffa Road.

In 1936 Elia was called to Aleppo to meet a woman the authorities thought might be his older sister. She recognized him immediately by a scar on his forehead. She was his only relative to survive the tragedy. While in Aleppo he met and married a young woman and together they returned to Jerusalem.

Just before the War of Independence in 1948, he was warned by a British policeman of the fighting about to begin. He took his archive and stored it in the family home. There it remained for many years until 1989, when his daughter-in-law decided to clean the attic and found thousands of old glass and silver nitrate plates with images of Jerusalem and Transjordan during the Mandate period. These rediscovered images won critical acclaim and proved invaluable to archaeologists and architects when restoring old, damaged buildings. In 1998 Elia's son Kevork published a collection of his father's work called *Jerusalem through My Father's Eyes*.

Elia died in April 1999 but his passion for photography has been passed on to his son and grandson Elia, who manage the gallery and the archive. Three generations of his family have between them captured seventy-five years of the life of an ever-changing city.

Elia's story is one of many in Israel demonstrating the triumph of hope over adversity. His legacy remains for future generations to enjoy and the gallery is a fitting tribute to a brave and courageous man who, in spite of everything he suffered, took such memorable and often serene images.

A nostalgic reminder of times past when life was simpler.

Artic Man

Artic Man on Herzliya beach

For those of you who visited Tel Aviv and other Israeli coastal towns in the early fifties, there is no doubt you will remember the "Artic" man.

Every day he trudged across the sand with his icebox slung over his shoulder, selling his ice lollies (popsicles) on a stick – chocolate, banana or lemon flavored. Nothing sophisticated like today's wrapped cones of ice cream, with nuts and whatever else you fancy stuck on top. No, this was simply an ice on a stick to cool you down while you sunned yourself on the beach.

Much has happened since the first Artic Man ventured forth – probably sixty years ago – but he is still there today, the same as ever, calling out his wares, *"Ani holech!"* (I'm going!), "Buy now before I leave." Of course today it will not be the original vendor – but it could well be the "Son of Artic Man" or even by now "Grandson of Artic Man." The boxes he carries say Nestlé's instead of Artic, but the principle is the same.

A nostalgic reminder of times past when life was simpler.

Surprisingly, however, there is today a thriving trade on eBay for original Artic Eskimo key rings. But the most touching website is one where you can contribute from ten to one hundred dollars to buy ices for Israel's soldiers – "Show them you care and give them a moment's relief from the heat by sending them Ice Lollies." Who can refuse such a request!

Suleiman was everything I expected, a charming, warm, generous and courteous host.

Bedouin Hospitality

Our host, Sheikh Suleiman

Desert hospitality is legendary, dating back to the earliest times when it was imperative for nomadic people to host and be hosted. For the host, this was how he received news of what was going on in the world, and for the guest it was a means of survival in a harsh environment.

During travels with Alon, my guide, we were invited to visit his old friend Sheik Suleiman for lunch. Suleiman, from the most important Bedouin tribe in Israel, worked for the British government during the Mandate period and later for the Israeli government, collecting taxes in the Negev. Today he lives in a Bedouin village with his extended family but has exchanged his tent for a permanent concrete structure.

Alon was at pains to explain their traditions and in particular their eating behavior. Bedouin never use utensils. They eat with their fingers, but only those of the right hand – *never* the left hand, this being reserved for *other*, more earthy bodily functions.

"You must eat," said Alon, "with three fingers of the right hand and the thumb, with little finger tucked into your palm. Take food from the communal dish, but never allow your fingers to touch your lips." My first challenge was to keep my little finger tucked into the palm of my hand, something I found utterly impossible in spite of practicing for six weeks with my finger taped to my palm.

The day arrived. We reached Suleiman's home – a simple cement building with small windows overlooking the desert, and cushions scattered around the perimeter of the room. Outside it was 40 degrees centigrade. Inside it was even hotter because a blazing wood fire was alight in the center of the room.

Bedouin food

Salman, a village elder, welcomed us by playing on a one-stringed instrument while we sat watching our host as he prepared coffee. This ritual involved putting coffee beans into a circular wooden container and pounding them with a long decorative pole. The rhythmic sound this made was a traditional means of informing neighbors that he had guests. Once roasted, the beans with the addition of cardamom seeds were heated in water, poured into a vessel and handed around. Somehow they missed me, which was a relief as I haven't drunk coffee since 1966 when the Brazilians increased the price and I went on a one-woman protest. (No one noticed – either the protest or the fact that I did not drink any coffee with the Sheikh.)

Next an enormous dish containing mountains of rice, vegetables and chicken was ceremoniously brought in. Everyone began taking handfuls of food, rolling it around and lifting it to their mouths. I started hesitatingly – found a pita bread and tried to fill it neatly with rice and vegetables – utterly impossible with one hand. I cannot describe the mess I got into. Food scattered everywhere, on my clothes and the cushions. Without thinking I found myself licking the greasy fingers of my *left* hand – and recoiled in horror when I realized what I was doing.

You need to understand, I was brought up in a middle-class Jewish home with Mother constantly admonishing me, "Don't eat with your fingers!" "Don't mess with your food!" But here I had to do precisely the opposite to be socially acceptable.

I sat opposite Suleiman to watch carefully how the "expert" did it. He lifted his right hand slowly and deliberately, placed it carefully in his inside pocket and to my surprise pulled out an enormous tablespoon, with which he began to eat. With the other hand he took out his iPhone and carried on a lengthy conversation.

I repressed a smile. I had been trying for weeks to perfect my eating technique, while here was our host, tucking in with a huge spoon. It was comforting to know that at least some of today's modern conveniences have been adopted into his lifestyle.

Suleiman was everything I expected, a charming, warm, generous and courteous host. I am not sure that I lived up to his ideal as a guest.

My experience confirmed one thing, however: to continue to be overly fastidious, and always use cutlery.

500 million birds fly over Israel twice a year

Bird Migration

The Huleh Valley, Israel

Israel is a bird lover's paradise. It is located on the Syrian-African Rift, which covers forty-two hundred miles from Mozambique to Turkey and is a major flight path for migrating birds.

Twice a year, five hundred million birds cross Israel's airspace. Scientists do not know for certain how birds navigate such lengthy routes, yet manage to return to the same place each year. This phenomenon was observed by the prophet Jeremiah, "Even the stork in the sky knows her appointed seasons, and the dove, the swift and the thrush observe the time of their migration" (Jeremiah 8:7).

Migrating birds fall in two groups. The larger ones – storks, cranes and pelicans – travel in flocks and seek thermals in which they can glide.

The other group, the passerines, are smaller birds that feed voraciously to double their weight before traveling. They flap their wings vigorously, using energy stored in their bodies to fly the shortest route possible.

The government of Israel is committed to supporting birds and in April 2012 pledged an additional $10.3 million toward funding the nation's network of birding centers. One major sanctuary is near Eilat. Storks and other large birds stop here to refuel, rest and recover before continuing their journey.

At the Jerusalem Bird Observatory workers and volunteers attach identification bands to around twelve thousand birds each year. This en-

Cranes reflected in the Huleh lake

ables ornithologists to track the birds' movements and learn about their behavior.

Apart from the visiting birds, Israel has more than 270 local species living in a variety of climatic conditions, from snow-covered mountains in the north to arid desert in the south.

Birds are a major attraction for both tourists and locals, with education in schools being a high priority as are the wide range of birding activities throughout the country.

One extraordinary sight is the cranes' annual arrival at the Huleh Valley in the Galilee. I saw for myself forty thousand cranes strutting, squawking and feeding, totally oblivious to our presence. Their food is provided by farmers and other organizations that help to deter birds from destroying crops and raiding local fish farms.

The preservation of all birds is central to Israel's nature conservationists. One species, the Griffon Vulture, was in danger of extinction, partially as a result of eating poisoned carcasses. Accordingly, breeding centers were established and chicks were successfully bred and released into the wild. Feeding stations were set up and the vultures soon learned where to obtain food. Their numbers are now slowly increasing.

Some vultures are ringed and carry GPS transmitters, allowing scientists to follow their travels. One vulture, named R65, unwittingly became the center of a major outcry in Saudi Arabia. He was "captured" in the Arabian desert and "arrested" by Saudi security forces who, on seeing the metal ring etched with the words "Tel Aviv University," claimed he was an Israeli spy.

Israeli bird arrested by Saudis as spy

It was only after the intervention of a Saudi prince, who realized the bird was not in fact a "Zionist infiltrator," that the bird was released to continue its travels. This event took place barely weeks after another incident, when a giant shark was found attacking tourists in the Red Sea. The local Egyptian governor suspected that it was acting on behalf of the Mossad. I understand that the shark was not apprehended.

Even more recently (August 2015) it was reported in the *Times* that a "spying dolphin" from Israel had been caught by Hamas. No photographic evidence has so far been produced to support their claim. However who knows? Recent evidence has shown that dolphins demonstrate very sophisticated traits of social learning and great intelligence. We know that we have bulls, bears and sharks in the world of high finance so why not dolphins in the world of espionage?

Forty thousand cranes arrive each year to the Huleh Valley, where food awaits them.

One udder thing, camel milk has ten times the amount of iron as cow's milk.

A proud camel

Camel – The Ship of the Desert

It is said that the camel is a horse designed by a committee, the implication being that group decision making will inevitably result in something badly constructed. In this case, it cannot be further from the truth – the camel is a highly intelligent animal, brilliantly adapted to its harsh environment.

It is the one-humped variety that is seen dotting the landscape in the Negev Desert of Israel. The Bedouin own most of these animals that traditionally were absolutely essential to their nomadic way of life. Imagine the Silk Route or the Spice Route without a camel train – impossible.

An indication of how central the animal is to their existence lies in the fact that the Bedouin have ninety-nine names for a camel describing, among other things, its age, condition, breed, shape and suitability for a particular job. My friend Alon has a list of a hundred but it is said that this can even reach into the thousands!

Called the "ships of the desert," camels could not have been better built for this purpose. Able to travel long distances with heavy loads, they can go without water or food for days and then drink a hundred liters in ten minutes when they get the opportunity. They have developed several methods of dealing with both high and low temperatures and can eat just about any vegetation with their leathery mouths and tongues.

Their skin is utilized for making shoes, bags

and saddles and their bones for jewelry and utensils. Their dung is burned as fuel. Nothing is wasted. One udder thing, they provide milk that has proven to be highly nutritious, having ten times the amount of iron as cows' milk, with claims that it can alleviate or even cure many illnesses.

Camel cigarettes have been on the market for years – I am not sure which part of the camel is used in this process. Camel milk chocolate, however, is marketed widely, as are camel skincare products, and camel milk ice cream burst onto the UK market in August 2011 as a deluxe specialty (£6 per scoop).

On reflection, if the camel was designed by a committee, I think they did a pretty good job.

Sheikh with a baby camel

Photo: Hanan Getraide

A Caring Society

Caring for an elderly man in a wheelchair

Nowhere in the world do I feel personally safer than in Israel. Some may express disbelief after reading the tabloids, but it is true.

Gang culture does not exist in Israel. To confront a group of teenagers in the street, an occasion for apprehension in London, is of no consequence in Tel Aviv.

Should there be a fracas in the street and you need help, everyone will come to your assistance without hesitation – Arabs, Druze, Christians and Jews, even old ladies wielding handbags. People look out for each other, not like some other countries where they are afraid to get involved, and where the police advise nonintervention in the event you might be injured going to someone's aid. When someone is attacked in London, people look away – they don't like to interfere.

Maybe this is the difference – Israelis love to interfere and in just about everything. In 1998, Israel established a law stating "anyone who can help another who is in sudden and serious danger, without risking himself – should do so." In England, "If you see a child drowning in a paddling pool there is no obligation for you to save it" (we speak here of legalities, not ethics). Similarly in the United States there is no general duty to come to the rescue of another – a person cannot be held liable for doing nothing while another person is in peril.

A friend's octogenarian mother fell down on the corner of Broadway and 34th street in New York. Not a single person came to her aid. Even medics will not assist as everyone there is afraid of insurance claims or legal action against them if they become involved.

In Israel, "helping" is at all levels. On buses passengers get on at the front entrance and buy their ticket from the driver. If someone boards through the middle door – usually mothers with strollers – they hand their fare to the person in front, who in turn hands it to another and so on until it reaches the driver. He produces a ticket or change, which is then sent back down the bus from one to another. This is the norm.

Some buses in Israel bear the inscription "You shall stand up before the aged and show deference to the old" – a quote from Leviticus intended to encourage courtesy among passengers.

A friend's son was alighting from a bus when his lunch box got trapped in the closing door as the bus began to depart. He would not let go of it. The whole bus erupted. Everyone screamed at the driver to stop and then some of the passengers insisted on taking the child to the hospital to check that he was OK.

I had an amusing encounter on a bus in Jerusalem recently. I saw the bus coming and rushed to get on. In doing so I failed to check whether I had loose change, and found that I only had a two-hundred-shekel note in my purse. The fare was 3.50 NIS. The driver looked very irritated and chastised me, saying I should have checked before I got on. I apologized profusely, saying that I would search my bag just in case any small change was lurking around.

I found nothing except one shekel and an unopened packet of mints. I decided to offer this to him, explaining that I hated not paying my debts. He burst out laughing and gave me a bus ticket but handed back the mints. I stood my ground and insisted he keep them as a gift from me (value

in all: NIS 4). I told him that every time he ate one he would remember me, and that, as I am a writer, I would use this incident as part of a story. I told him that on one occasion in London I remember being shown off a bus when I didn't have the right money! He was shocked! He is of course now waiting for the book to be published so that he can read about his heroic actions.

Kindnesses like this are common in Israel. A few years ago my father died while on holiday in Netanya. I ordered a taxi to go there from Jerusalem. A young driver took me, first to the hotel where my father had died and then to the hospital where Dad's body had been taken. Five hours later the driver brought me back to Jerusalem and refused to take payment for the time he had spent with me. He was loving and supportive and like a member of the family.

One of the most profound experiences in recent years was the public reaction to the release of Gilad Schalit, the young Israeli soldier kidnapped and held by Hamas for five and a half years. After constant public pressure and negotiations he was eventually returned to his parents in October 2011, this solitary soldier being exchanged for 1,027 Arab prisoners held in Israeli jails. At the moment of his release everyone was glued to the television and there wasn't a dry eye in the country. It was as though he was the son, brother or friend of everyone.

Sometimes this country can be irritating, but at its best it is truly like one large, warm, enveloping blanket.

Casino de Paris, Jerusalem

A handshake across the bar

A Casino de Paris is not something you would expect to find in a corner of the Mahane Yehuda market in downtown Jerusalem. But here it is – a bar, complete with Toulouse Lautrec posters and atmospheric décor.

This was the brainchild of two friends, Eli Mizrachi and Sha'anan Street, who restored it in the same building where, during the British Mandate, flourished a bar of the same name patronized by British officers and the sons of wealthy Arabs.

The original building was constructed in 1910. Ten years later a small hotel, the Casino de Paris, was opened at the back. It was a combination of a respectable British Officer's club and a

not-so-respectable brothel, where patrons drank and were entertained by ladies of the night. A small orchestra played the tango and paso doble on the rooftop, where couples would dance under the stars. It is not difficult to imagine the atmosphere of romance and sophistication in this exotic setting. Apparently, whisky, gin and even Guinness were imported to the Casino de Paris specially for their customers, the British soldiers serving in Palestine.

The Brits, who did things in style, employed the services of renowned architect Charles Ashbee. He had a colorful background, being the son of Henry Spencer Ashbee, a bibliophile and writer

> A small orchestra
> played the tango
> on the rooftop,
> where couples
> would dance
> under the stars.

mostly known for his huge collection of erotic literature and works by Cervantes (donated to the British Museum on his death). His mother was Jewish and a keen supporter of the suffragette movement.

Charles was an enthusiastic advocate of the Arts and Crafts movement of William Morris and influenced by other thinkers and activists of the day such as John Ruskin. From 1919 to 1922 he acted as advisor to the British Mandate administration in Palestine, overseeing building works and protecting historical sites.

One of his ideas was to plan a garden to en-circle the Old City, to place the ancient walls in a quasi-rural setting. During this period the British also determined that all buildings in Jerusalem must be faced with local Jerusalem stone (limestone and dolomite) – an ordinance which is still in force, contributing a great deal to the unique character of the city. Another project of the time was to develop the market into the colonial ideal of an oriental bazaar.

The hotel plied its trade until 1948 when, with the establishment of the State of Israel and the departure of the British, the building and the area fell into disrepair. It remained this way until Mizrachi and his team lovingly restored it to its former glory, keeping the original tiled floors and whatever else of character remained.

Every evening the courtyard in front of the Casino is packed to capacity in the heart of the market, sandwiched between vegetable and fruit vendors and a bakery. Ashbee and his colleagues would have heartily approved.

The reestablishment of the brothel is, as far as I know, not yet on the agenda.

Cats

A stray – the eyes have it…

During the Mandate period in Palestine (1917–1948), the British developed infrastructure, architecture and a solid legal system, much of which remains today. Another legacy that they inadvertently left is the proliferation of cats in Israel.

The British, being great cat lovers, brought pets from home to deal with the rodents they faced in the Holy Land. On returning to the United Kingdom they failed to take their feline friends back with them. Result – abandoned cats left to roam and breed unchecked. Today it is estimated that there are between one and two million feral cats in the country.

This overpopulation of stray cats is a major problem. Ministerial guidelines on feeding them were drafted and in 2009 a major pet association launched a campaign to distribute twenty-seven hundred feeding bowls in the Rothschild area of Tel Aviv. Detractors complained that this merely drew more cats to the area and feeding them curtailed their natural instinct to hunt. Cat lovers claim the animals serve a useful purpose by hunting snakes and rodents, but evidence shows that cats have a distinct preference for birds and protected species, seriously upsetting the balance of nature. The Rufous Bush Robin, a beautiful songbird, is one example of a species that has almost been eradicated.

It is complex to untangle the arguments for and against. If you love animals, you help them.

If not, you want them removed. The passion and dedication this issue raises is extraordinary. A band of elderly ladies throughout the country devote their lives to cats, often themselves suffering abuse from neighbors. One woman took out a loan of NIS 100,000 to fund her obsession. The cats stayed. Her husband left. Is it only the mature and female of the species that have this urge?

One of the sweetest stories I heard was from a friend who had just completed his army service. During his time on the base everyone was issued with a written directive regarding cats.

1. You must not touch the cats.
2. You must not feed them.
3. You must never, under any circumstances, give them names.

This is quite understandable really. After all how can any self-respecting army condone fraternization, or caternization in this instance.

For centuries man systematically destroyed almost all the wild cats in the Middle East. Perhaps what we face today is fair retribution for their actions. Large wild cats gone. Small wild cats came. We shall just have to accept these feline foragers yowling at night, occupying our best upholstered garden chairs to have their litters and leaving little deposits in the flower beds. Is this a CATastrophe?

Six cats on a refuse container – their favorite feeding / meeting place

Courtesy of Caviar Galilee, Kibbutz Dan.

Caviar

Yigal Ben Zvi holding a sturgeon

Seventy-three years ago had you suggested to the founders of socialist Kibbutz Dan that one day they would be producing caviar, arguably the most extravagant capitalistic product on the market, they would have laughed in your face.

Today, however, things have changed – serendipitously, as a result of the massive immigration to Israel in the 1990s when Gorbachev allowed Soviet Jews to leave the USSR.

At that time Kibbutz Dan already had years of experience in trout farming, but, facing stiff competition, decided to branch out into breed-ing sturgeon to satisfy the fishy tastes of the new immigrants.

In 1998 they purchased fertilized osetra eggs from Russia and began raising sturgeon. In 2002 caviar prices were rising internationally because of a total embargo on fishing in the Caspian Sea due to overexploitation. Previously 95 percent of the world's caviar production had come from there.

The kibbutz then wisely decided to divert their activity toward producing caviar. They sorted the male from the female fish, a procedure that can only be determined at the age of four years. The

The market
price for
caviar can
be as much
as £2,400
per pound.

males were raised for "meat" and the females for egg production. Under normal circumstances females do not mature sexually until fourteen or fifteen years of age, but Israeli experts developed techniques whereby the fish could produce eggs at six to eight years.

Kibbutz Dan is blessed with having a plentiful supply of pure spring water. They are thus able to replenish their fish tanks twice daily, which helps to ensure a high-quality product.

I was told that each female can produce between four and thirteen pounds of eggs, which seems a huge amount, but the fish do grow to quite a few feet in length. In 2011 the kibbutz sold three tons of caviar but aims to increase output to nine tons per year from their forty thousand sturgeon. Nowadays the market price for caviar can be as much as £2,400 per pound.

Today there has been a worldwide reversal in caviar production, with 90 percent coming from fish farms and only 10 percent from nature. According to experts there is no difference in the quality.

When I visited the kibbutz I met Chalil – an Alawite Muslim who has worked there for over thirty years and is part of the extended kibbutz family. He is responsible for looking after the sterilized rooms where the eggs are extracted and packed. He explained how small quantities of eggs can be "milked" from the fish to check their size and quality and how these eggs can also

be used for breeding purposes. The fish are not harmed at all by this process.

Every story reveals another one. Chalil told me how the village of Ghajar where he was born, close to Kibbutz Dan, had been under dispute since the nineteenth century as to whether it was in Syria or Lebanon. It is today part of Israel since they took control of the Golan Heights. Its residents have full Israeli citizenship, receive all benefits and speak fluent Hebrew. Most of them, however, consider themselves Syrians and part of the minority Alawite community.

Jordan, however, continues to dispute Syria's claim, stating that it was only as a result of poor British mapmaking that it came under Syrian control. Chalil told me how only a week earlier the village received yet another visit from the International Red Cross trying to find a solution, and this had gone on for years.

I asked him where he considered he lived, whereupon he looked down at the ground and said, "Where I was born is where I live, whatever anyone wants to call it."

One issue facing Israel's fish farmers is that sturgeon has never been accepted as kosher. Maimonides, the eminent twelfth-century rabbinic scholar, approved the kosher status of the "esturgeon," but it is not clear if this is the same species as today's sturgeon.

Professor Berta Levavi-Sivan of the Hebrew University disagrees with today's rabbinical ban on sturgeon and maintains that the fish is kosher as it has scales, albeit small ones not discernible to the naked eye, as well as fins. Meanwhile most of Kibbutz Dan's output is exported to Europe and North America rather than being sold in Israel.

No doubt the jury will be out on the kosher/nonkosher issue for some time, but the caviar, acknowledged by top chefs as being of superlative quality, should be enough to support the socialist lifestyle of Kibbutz Dan for many years to come.

Photo: Ester Beck. Courtesy of Benyamini Contemporary Ceramics Center.

Ceramic Art

Maud Friedland ceramics

Talk to anyone today about a potter and the image that springs to most minds is that of a bespectacled teenage wizard, the creation of J.K. Rowling. But this would never occur to me as for years I have been completely fascinated by potters and pots – and Israel has a wealth of ceramics dating back to prebiblical times.

One of the oldest known discoveries was excavated in a late Bronze Age *tel* at Lachish, where archaeologists found raw materials, tools for making pots, stones for burnishing them, and even some complete vessels. For years Arabs in Hebron and Gaza made domestic pots, employing techniques passed from father to son, but contemporary Israeli ceramics began in the 1930s thanks to the influence of three immigrants known as the mothers of Israeli ceramics.

Hava Samuel arrived from Germany in 1933 and immediately opened a primitive studio with no water supply and a kiln fired on kerosene. In spite of this she managed to produce items from local clay "hoping to educate the public taste" which she considered "beyond the pale."

That same year Hedwig Grossman arrived. An intellectual, she aspired to develop the potters' craft in Israel, but the kibbutz factory she established to make functional ware was beset with arguments as to whether it was an ideologically appropriate occupation for a kibbutz. The third "mother," Hanna Zunz Harag, was responsible for starting the Israeli ceramics industry in Haifa.

Many potters have followed in their footsteps and certain themes have emerged as singularly Israeli: a love of landscape reflecting the hues and

The processes are meditative, spiritual, time consuming and unpredictable.

rough textures of the desert; indigenous plant life – the sabra, pomegranate and olive; and the use of organic materials combined with clay.

Other common motifs are echoes of Arab, Bauhaus, Mandate and Turkish architecture – Israel being the point where East meets West and so many civilizations have left their imprint. In addition, the frequent wars and social upheavals in the region have each made their mark in the creative vocabulary of the potters.

Archaeology too has had a profound impact. Israeli museum collections testify to the creativity of artisans through the millennia. Today's potters absorb these images, develop their own styles and create new traditions of working with clay.

But the diversity of styles is wide ranging nowadays as Israelis travel abroad and attend residencies overseas. In turn, potters from those countries come to give workshops in Israel.

The Arts Institute at Tel Hai has been pivotal in encouraging this cross-fertilization, hosting an annual symposium attracting up to four hundred participants. Bezalel in Jerusalem, Neot Hakikar in the south and the Bet Benyamini Center in Tel Aviv have furthered the process.

I have collected pots since my teens. To hold a pot, feel its form and texture, appreciate the glaze or the marks made by the artist, much as one interprets brush marks on a canvas, is magical.

Potters are a special breed. They take a lump of clay, and from the very basic elements of our existence – water, fire and oxygen – transform it into something unique. The processes are meditative, spiritual, time consuming and unpredictable. The results can be inspiring.

The Bible has many references to the potter and his wheel as a metaphor for creation. God formed Adam from the clay of the earth. Man in turn took that same clay, produced functional objects and later, developed a sense of aesthetics to create artefacts that have given pleasure to many for generations.

Exhibition of contemporary ceramics, Bet Benyamini.

Photo: Shai Ben Efraim

Challah

Challah for Shabbat

Throughout the week Israelis eat their daily bread. When Friday comes, this staple is transformed into something extra special – challah, or Sabbath bread. For some reason it tastes so much better.

Every weekend, families buy or bake two special loaves for their Friday night meal and for two meals on the Sabbath. Two are required to remember the time when the Israelites wandered in the desert after their exodus from Egypt, and manna fell from heaven, but not on the Sabbath. Instead they received two portions the day before.

Challah has different shapes and sizes, all of which have symbolic meaning. The regular plaited version of four or seven strands symbolizes love, as it is said to resemble intertwined arms. Three strands can mean truth, peace and justice. The twelve-strand challah is called the Twelve Tribes' Challah, recalling the twelve tribes of Israel. Round shapes that have no beginning and no end are baked for the New Year as an expression of continuity. These can be circular twists or constructed resembling a turban, sprinkled with decorations for a festive effect.

When making challah a small portion of the dough is removed as a symbolic "tithe" for the priests. This practice dates back to biblical times and is considered a "mitzvah" or obligation. The rules on how to apply this are complex. Whether or not one has to make a blessing during the process depends on the precise size of the dough and four different rabbis will have four different opinions as to what constitutes the "correct" amount.

One says dough weighing 3lb. 10.8 oz. requires a blessing. For a bread weighing 2 lb. 11.4 oz. no blessing is required but a piece must still be removed. Below this there is no need to either bless it or take away anything – an exacting process that would seem to be enough to put anyone off, however this proves to be not the case.

I recently heard of a new trend that has taken hold in Israel among secular girls, the majority of whom do not usually keep the rules of the Sabbath. "*Hafrashat challah* parties" are held where they meet to learn about the bread-making process and in particular the commandment to separate a piece of the dough.

They believe that this mitzvah brings great merit to those who perform it. One young girl came to a session after she was diagnosed with cancer. She attended regularly and is convinced that it is following this commandment and reciting the blessing that keeps her healthy.

One woman recites the prayer; the rest respond with amen. For it is stated in the Talmud (*Berachot* 53b, *Nazir* 66) that the gates of heaven open for those who answer amen with all their might, even more than for those who actually recite the prayer. Among the Orthodox community there are some women who take their dough to the graveside of the Rambam (Maimonides) in Tiberias. They separate a piece and say the prayer in the belief that their requests to the Almighty are more likely to be answered.

Traditionally it was the role of the woman of the household to make the challah. One story goes that a newly married couple were eating their Shabbat meal together. The husband asks his wife, "Rivka, when are you going to start make challah like your mother?" To which she retorted, "When you start making dough like your father."

Curiously, however, in some households today the roles are reversing. The wife earns the money and the husband makes the challah. Perhaps some men have a better grasp of the maths involved, or maybe it gives rein to their creative urges. Also there is no question that the rhythmic quality of kneading dough can be a spiritual process, especially when one is doing it to welcome in the Sabbath.

All I remember as a child being told about bread making is that it was a very good way of cleaning one's hands. Later on I learned that other families used soap.

Making bread is a good way of cleaning one's hands. . .

Photo courtesy of Dafna Ben Yochanan.

The Choir and the Concert

My debut

In 2012 I was persuaded to sing in a concert at the Jerusalem Music Academy to raise money for the Ankor Girls Choir.

I first met them in 1988. I helped with their UK tour and saw them perform at the Eisteddfod Music Festival in Wales. As our Israeli choir mounted the stage there was a massive clap of thunder followed by a storm of biblical proportions. The marquee swayed precariously in the wind and was on the point of collapsing. After the choir's performance our ambassadorial party beat a hasty retreat as did I, struggling through

mud, gale force winds and torrential rain – an unforgettable occasion!

These girls, aged eleven to seventeen, look like any other group of teenagers – low-cut jeans revealing bare midriffs and long flowing hair which they toss back constantly and fiddle with endlessly. But appearances are deceptive – when they start to sing you hear the voices of angels as they achieve a level of musical professionalism that is, in their parlance, *"awesome!"*

Since then I have kept in touch with them, watching their progress. They recently performed

Obama's
hands were
so soft they
wondered
what kind of
hand cream
he used.

in Carmen at Masada and also sang for President Obama at Yad Vashem. He, being the consummate diplomat, shook hands with each one of them. Their impression was that he was "really fit and cool" and his hands were so soft they wondered what kind of hand cream he used.

In 2012 they were the only Israeli choir invited to take part in a major competition in Ohio. Twenty thousand singers were to attend including one hundred choirs from China alone. After the initial excitement of receiving the invitation, it sadly dawned on them that they could not afford to go. On hearing this I contacted several generous friends in London and between us we raised almost enough to get them there.

Ankor won a gold medal. They also won a silver medal for liturgical music. Their conductor, Dafna Ben Yochanan, expressed disappointment that it was only silver, to which I pointed out that for a Jewish choir singing Christian music they did pretty well to get even a silver! Zubin Mehta wrote a congratulatory letter on their remarkable achievement. I was bursting with pride and so happy to have had a small part in helping them to get there.

And now back to the concert. Dafna had urged me to take part to help raise the remaining money they needed for their trip. You have to understand that until six years ago I had never once opened my mouth to sing and never given a thought to performing. I had taken the singing exams at the Guildhall School of Music but in my view this did not constitute sufficient experience to stand before a real live audience.

The day of the concert arrived. My four solos included the "Habanera" from Carmen, "Send In The Clowns" by Sondheim and "Where Corals Lie" by Edward Elgar. Dafna also insisted that I perform something in Hebrew.

She selected Tango Kfar Saba – a pastiche from the 1930s by poet Natan Alterman. It was a love story based on a farming community and included tender phrases such as "My heart is like an incubator," "The cows moo in the cowshed," and the even more passionate "The gates of the farm are locked because of foot and mouth disease." Not the usual romantic repertoire but it did add a number of useful phrases to my Hebrew vocabulary.

My pianist Paul and I waited backstage for a couple of hours. Suddenly he announced, "Oh no! We've forgotten to practice walking on!" This was news to me. I had assumed that "walking on" was simply "walking on" but apparently not. I asked him to explain. "Just remember," he said, "you must walk with dignity." I told him politely that I don't usually do dignity, but nevertheless when the moment came I entered the stage so regally that Queen Elizabeth of England could not have done better.

The concert was fine, so everyone said. I am not sure about the voice, but I can tell you that I walked on quite magnificently and wonder if I have missed my vocation.

Perhaps if I had started singing when I was eleven – the age, incidentally, when I was rejected for the school choir – maybe I would not feel the same trepidation about exposing myself to a discerning public. We shall never find out.

Commemorating Yom Hazikaron (Remembrance Day)

Pedestrians in Emek Refaim showing their respect

Yom Hazikaron is Israel's Day of Remembrance for those who fell in active service defending their country. It takes place on the day prior to Independence Day. All over Israel religious, military and civil ceremonies are attended by families and friends, many of whom have lost someone. Memorial candles are lit in public places such as schools, army camps and synagogues and flags fly at half-mast.

By law, all places of entertainment have to close on the eve of Yom Hazikaron. Schools and other educational institutions focus on the solemnity of the day. Radio and TV networks show special programs suitable for the occasion.

Israel is a very small country. Everyone is touched in some way by having lost a close family member or friend, Israel having fought nine wars since its establishment in 1948.

Life is precious for Jews, and to lose even one soldier in battle is a tragedy shared by all. There is no other time when the country draws so closely together like one large family. The gravity of the day is palpable, but what impresses most is what happens at 11 A.M.

Last year I went out to the new Bridge of Strings located at the entrance to Jerusalem, designed by Spanish architect Santiago Calatrava. It was a good vantage point from where to take my pictures and to view the main highway, always crowded with several lanes of traffic.

At eleven o'clock I arrived and saw how at this appointed hour not only did every single vehicle stop but drivers got out of their cars and stood by them silently for two minutes as an act of remembrance.

This year I went to Emek Refaim Street in Jerusalem. Again every car stopped, and in addition every pedestrian stood still, head bowed, in memory of friends and comrades lost. Their shared grief was pervasive.

It was chillingly emotional, deeply moving and totally unforgettable.

Chillingly emotional, deeply moving and totally unforgettable.

Traffic standing still on Yom Hazikaron

For some unaccountable reason it is now "cool" to go to singsongs.

Communal Singing

Street singer with audience, near the market, Tel Aviv

Israeli folk music began in the early twentieth century and in those pioneering days comprised patriotic themes about "the land." Poems of that era were set to music, as were specially written pieces by performers such as Naomi Shemer, considered to be the first lady of Israeli song and poetry.

Over the decades this style of music became unfashionable, but during the last few years it has had a renaissance, particularly with the young. For some unaccountable reason it is now "cool" to go to singsongs where melodies from the bygone era of one's parents or grandparents are reprised. This rebirth is a bizarre phenomenon. Perhaps it

is a response to the political pressures of today and allows participants to indulge in an evening of pure nostalgia and a chance to escape from the harsh reality of the modern world.

Israelis have always loved getting together to sing, whether in public halls, private homes, on the kibbutz, around a barbecue or on the beach ("*kumzitz*"). Anywhere will do and anyone can come.

Once a week every Thursday at the Mamilla Mall in Jerusalem I stand for two hours spellbound, watching a packed audience of all ages join in with a professional singer. At first all the songs sound to me much like listening to the

Eurovision song contest entries from Croatia or Iceland, but suddenly they become familiar and I find myself humming along.

Singing is the most wonderful feel-good activity. Like taking a happy pill. It simply doesn't matter whether one has a good voice or not. Israelis get together and sing for the sheer exuberant joy of enjoying each other's company and sharing in a life-enriching activity.

They say nostalgia is a thing of the past – not at all! It is very much a thing of the present.

Children with street performer

Cornucopia of Times Past

Interior of Palestina

Located in the heart of the old Arab quarter of Jaffa is the flea market, or *shuk hapishpeshim*. On the ground floor of an old Ottoman building on Olei Tzion Street is Palestina. To call it a "shop" is a misnomer – it is more an experience, a journey back in time and a chance to be reacquainted with many of the things one remembers from childhood.

This veritable cornucopia is the creation of Amotz Yakobi – an Israeli whose whole life has been devoted to collecting. Over the years he has gathered thousands of items which today jostle for room and crowd the walls, shelves, ceiling and every available inch of floor space.

As a child he was a loner, given to walking in the fields near his home, along the tracks of what was once Palestine Railways. Here he found treasures, especially fossils embedded in the rocks that had been dumped there when they originally built the railway.

When he was six, he came across a small plate, lying on the ground in perfect condition. He did not know its history, nor could he read the English writing on its surface, but he knew instinctively that it had value. Forty-six years later, this piece, a plate from Palestine Railways, has pride of place in his home.

The world is made up of those who hoard and those who don't. I am in the latter category. Amotz is quite definitely in the former.

On leaving school he went to art college, qualified and decided to become a teacher, but soon realized that his true love lay in being surrounded by the ephemera of other people's lives and opened a shop to sell the items he had collected. He has a few golden rules. He only buys original items, preferably over a hundred years old, never replicas. He seeks any kind of functional objects and, in spite of his art training, is not interested in purely decorative or artistic pieces.

Tools and equipment hold a fascination for him, with his natural ability to understand how things work. Only 5 percent of anything he has was made in pre-1948 Israel. The rest comprises items brought to the country by the succession of immigrants who arrived from all corners of the globe.

The place gives the impression of utter chaos, but Amotz swears he knows where everything is. All items are priced but, unlike most market traders, he never bargains. Customers, he says, fall into two types. The first is the urbane, suited lawyer or accountant searching for a pen or a watch. He inspects everything critically and invariably asks for a discount. The second is the customer who picks up a tool, handles it with affection, buys it without a murmur and returns later to report how much pleasure it gives him. It

The world is made up of those who hoard and those who don't.

is encounters with this type that gives Amotz the most satisfaction.

I sat with him for a couple of hours. People arrived clutching bags from which emerged items that they have, sometimes reluctantly, decided to part with. Amotz, the consummate professional, knows the value of everything and deals sensitively with those handing over their "heirlooms."

Others entered unable to resist the opportunity to browse, commenting, "Look, my grandfather used to have one of these!" or "Wow, haven't seen something like this for ages!" To my surprise, absolutely everyone left him with a smile and words of appreciation – all this in a country not renowned for its courtesy.

Amotz, the armchair philosopher, believes his destiny in the world is to "fix things" but is not quite sure what needs fixing. What he has done, probably without realizing it, is to "fix" up his visitors with something unique – the chance to indulge in nostalgia, to escape from the frenzied activity of the modern world and linger for a brief moment in a bygone era.

Crossing the Road

Waiting for the lights to change, Tel Aviv

One of the most inappropriate adjectives one might use to describe an Israeli is *passive*. Argumentative, yes, self-opinionated, yes, emotional, yes. It was President Chaim Weizmann, the first head of state, who once said, "I head a nation of one million presidents."

Israelis tend not to obey rules. If there is a way of getting round them, they will find it. The only exception is when you see them waiting to cross the road at the traffic lights. There they stand, patiently, obediently, quietly, waiting for the "little green man" to appear. The road in each direction may be totally empty, with not a vehicle or policeman in sight, but they do not stir. Not until the green man gives them permission will they venture forth.

True, there is a heavy fine for jaywalking, but I believe this behavior indicates more than that. I like to think that it may be an urge to show solidarity with one's fellow man. Anyone who transgresses this pattern of behavior and crosses on red, as I do too often, is publicly reprimanded. Quite touching, really: this excitable race, in at least one area of its life, has a brief period of quietude.

> There they stand, patiently, obediently, quietly...

Drinking in Israel

Throughout the Bible there are copious references to the relationship between Jews and alcohol, focusing on the normative practice of drinking wine as part of Jewish ritual and celebration.

The centrality of wine in their lifestyle is one reason why Jews have a much lower level of alcoholism than other groups. It has an accepted role, partaken at every Sabbath meal and festivals. At the Passover meal four glasses must be drunk and on Purim Jews are exhorted to celebrate "until they cannot differentiate" between heroes and villains. Rabbinic commentaries however, say this must not be taken literally, and drinking should be moderate.

Jewish children see wine as a legitimate part of life, tasting it at an early age. But drinking to excess is severely frowned upon as it can lead to losing one's self-control.

In Israel social drinking has increased, blamed partially on the massive influx in the 1980s of one million immigrants from the former Soviet Union, where drinking was commonplace. For some time after their arrival, doctors in emergency wards in Israel were dealing with patients with unrecognized symptoms. It turned out to be alcoholism.

Today young people frequent bars where drink is freely available – something that never occurred in the past. In spite of this, a WHO project a few years ago confirmed that the per capita intake of alcohol in Israel is much lower than in most western countries due to social, cultural and genetic influences (Food and Agriculture Organization of the United Nations, "World Drink Trends," 2003). Scientific research has confirmed that Jews have inherited a gene predisposing them to lower alcohol consumption, with a reduced risk of alcohol dependency.

"Maybe if Jews drank more they might not worry so much about their health?"

A weekend night in any UK city sees unspeakably rowdy behavior when pubs close. The media is full of articles about teenagers who go out binge drinking with the sole purpose of getting "legless." This is regarded as the norm and a badge of honor, similar to the rite of passage in Ireland, where a father takes his teenage son out for the first time to drink him under the table as a sign of manhood. This undesirable face of drinking has not yet reached such levels in Israel, public drunkenness being considered unacceptable rather than amusing as it is in the United Kingdom and America.

I recently went to one of the newer entertainment areas in Jerusalem to take pictures of people out enjoying a drink. The only drinkers I found were a lone guy reading a book and having a pint, and a guy and his uncle having a chat over a beer. Hundreds of people eating, but no groups drinking. Obviously I was in the wrong place at the wrong time.

Having a drink

One function of jokes in society is the ability to highlight certain issues, but whereas hundreds exist about inebriated Irishmen, it is hard to find even one about a drunken Jew. But read this:

A Frenchman, a German and a Jew are lost in the desert, wandering for days. The Frenchman says, "I'm tired and thirsty. I must have a glass of wine." The German says, "I'm tired and thirsty. I must have a beer." The Jew says, "I'm tired and thirsty. I must have diabetes."

This, as you will realize, attests to Jewish abstinence, but underlines another Jewish trait – that of hypochondria. Maybe if Jews drank more they might not worry so much about their health?

Nir can toss the balls in the air and catch them while simultaneously beating a rhythm on his tray.

Tossing falafel

Falafel

Israel without falafel would be like England without fish and chips. Falafel did not come to Israel with any of the waves of immigrants, but was quickly adopted by them once they arrived. It originated from the Christian Coptic community in Egypt, who were not permitted to eat meat during certain holidays and invented falafel as a non-meat alternative. Highly nutritious, it comprises chickpeas or fava beans, which are pounded into a mix with spices and deep-fried.

Other Middle East countries have claimed it as their own. One such country is Lebanon, whose chefs excelled in May 2010 when they prepared 5.7 tons of falafel mix – the biggest ever. There have also been attempts to see who can make the big-

gest falafel ball. The winners to date are a group in the United States who made a 52.8 pound ball, more than three feet in circumference – an effort that they hope will gain them entry to the Guinness Book of Records. What strange things people do in their spare time!

Setting up a falafel stall in Israel was once one of the surefire ways of earning a decent living. Today there are thousands of kiosks, most of them claiming to serve "the best" falafel around and run by their own "falafel king."

Falafel has spawned a group of expert practitioners – super falafel makers – like Nir from Afula who can toss the balls in the air and catch them in a pita while simultaneously beating a rhythm on his metal tray. Or Meir, who performs similar juggling skills in Beersheba. I stood and watched him serve nonstop for twenty minutes – producing each filled pita in around ten seconds flat.

So choose your falafel maker; have the pita filled at breakneck speed demonstrating super aerodynamic skills and crammed with hummus, tehina and every available pickle and salad. All you have to do now is eat it.

What amazes me is that Israel, whose scientists have entered into the world of high technology with outstanding success, has never managed to devise a way of eating this national food without most of it running up your arm or dropping on the floor.

There is a fortune to be made here by some astute inventor who can manufacture a disposable liquid-proof holder that would make eating this a less messy and more aesthetic experience. Or perhaps that would spoil the fun?

Here it is - your falafel

Caracal, a mixed gender battalion has 70 percent female soldiers.

Female Fighting Force

A caracal

Women in the land of Israel have long played an active role in defending their country. During the Mandate period they fought under fire for organizations such as Hashomer, Haganah and the Palmach who declared, "Our doors are open to any man or woman prepared and trained to fulfil the obligations of national defense."

During WW2, four thousand women joined the British forces in Palestine. One woman who became a truck driver said that it was considered "the height of boldness" to undertake such a job at that time. With the outbreak of the War of Independence in 1948 women comprised almost a third of the Palmach, several achieving the rank of commander. The military authorities, however, subsequently banned women from engaging in combat, largely because of the personal risk should they be captured. Instead they fulfilled other essential roles.

Today Israel is one of the few countries in the world with compulsory military service for women. The time they serve depends on their age at entry, but is less than the three years that men have to serve. Conscription is from age eighteen to twenty-four, with exemptions for those who are married, pregnant or mothers. The religiously observant can opt for National Service and work with children, the elderly, and many other welfare causes.

I became interested in the role of women in the Israeli army while researching the question of sexism. The younger generation I spoke with maintained that it hardly exists. These were mostly female officers whose duties involved training male soldiers. The response from the older women was not quite so positive – understandable perhaps, as they served a while ago when attitudes were different.

In 2012, retired brigadier general Yehudit Grisaro's response to this issue was "I never met a man who would take the risk," and, of course, in the army sexism is illegal. Today Yehudit is vice president at El Al Israel Airlines. When she left the army her place was taken by Orna Barvibay, the first female in the history of the Israeli army to become a major general, in 2011.

Elinor Joseph, another outstanding soldier, was the first Arab woman to serve publicly in a combat role. An exemplary cadet, she worked as a medic in the Caracal unit, established in 2000, and named after a wildcat that roams the Negev desert where the unit is based.

Caracal, a mixed-gender battalion, comprises 70 percent females of Jewish and Arab descent. Today it aims to incorporate women into combat roles (the earlier ban having been lifted). The battalion sets a high medical profile for their recruits who undergo four months of basic and two months of advanced training. They engage in hard physical work with the Givati Brigade and specialize in handling machine guns, mortars and grenades.

They operate along the Egyptian border, preventing the infiltration of terrorists. This battalion produced the first female officer to command a sniper platoon, Second Lieutenant Noy. In 2013 Lieutenant Amit Danon was added to this illustrious list when she became a platoon commander.

But it is not only in Caracal that women have achieved success. They are also active in the Combat Engineering Brigade, entering enemy territory to neutralize live weapons during battle. Others work in Oketz Unit K9, with dogs trained to sniff out explosives and track down terrorists and escaped criminals.

By 2012 twenty-seven women had graduated as fighter pilots in the Israel Air Force. In the navy women are "manning" (may we still use that word?) armed motorboats to protect maritime bases. Part of their job involves diving under naval vessels to check that no mines or explosives have been attached. Hardly a job for the fainthearted!

Researching this story made me realize how dramatically attitudes have changed over the years. When I left school in the United Kingdom (at sixteen) I was supposed to become a secretary or hairdresser and find a husband. Going to university was rarely an option. This I eventually did as a mature student of thirty-two with three sons in tow. To think of going into the army simply never entered our terms of reference.

It is generally accepted that certain roles are best filled by men because of their greater physical capabilities. However, today more than 92 percent of all IDF jobs are open to women, half of the army lieutenants are women, and 13 percent of these move on to become lieutenant colonel. Without doubt these remarkable young women are leading the way in challenging traditional stereotypes of females in our society. King Solomon asked "A woman of valour who will find?" (Proverbs 31:10). The IDF has certainly provided one answer.

Egyptian hieroglyphs depict fish growing in ponds four thousand years ago

Fish Farming

Conversation piece

I was born and grew up in Manchester, a grey industrial city in Lancashire, renowned for its football club and the fact that it rains a lot. The rain was responsible for the establishment of several important industries, mainly cotton spinning which later developed into manufacturing of raincoats and umbrellas, mostly by Jewish entrepreneurs.

Having accepted damp and drizzle as the norm, Israel was a shock to my system. It is a country with a serious lack of rain that, contrary to my expectations, has led to the creation of one unexpectedly successful industry, that of aquaculture.

Embarrassingly, my knowledge of fish extends not much further than the "gefilte" variety, in spite of the fact that fishing is the main recreational activity in Britain. On one memorable occasion

I nervously ventured into a river in Weardale, dressed for the occasion in my Wellington boots. There I stood hopefully for six hours but didn't catch anything at all except for a heavy cold.

Fish farming, however, was well known in ancient times. Egyptian hieroglyphs depict fish growing in ponds four thousand years ago, but the start of fish farming in today's Israel took place in the 1940s when Kibbutz Dan imported freshwater trout eggs from the United States and carp were brought to an experimental farm near Acre.

Today there are three governmental fish-research stations in Israel. At Ginossar I learned that one of their main activities is to replace the declining numbers of fish in Lake Kinneret. Each year millions of fingerlings are put back to replenish the stock. At one time the lake had twenty-three species, but many have disappeared and others are threatened due to overfishing, climate changes and predation by migrating birds.

One of the most surprising developments is the extent to which aquaculture has taken off in the arid Negev region in the south – one of the driest areas in the world with virtually no rainfall.

In was here that Professor Arieh Issar discovered a mass of underground geothermal water dating back millions of years. This water is 98 degrees Fahrenheit, has a 10 percent saline content, and is brackish and completely free of pollutants. As such it is perfect for use in fish farms. The water repels diseases, the fish grow faster because of the salinity and there are no heating costs. After circulating in the fish farms this water is then used for irrigation of crops such as tomatoes, watermelons, grapes, jojoba and olives, with the added benefit that organic waste from the fish makes perfect fertilizer for these crops.

More than ten intensive fish farms have been built in the Negev. Constructed as large plastic "bubbles," these farms keep the water and air temperature constant throughout the year – essential considering the extreme summer heat and the freezing winter nights. Yields are up to thirty-five times higher than those of fish grown in typical outdoor ponds. Another major advantage of this system is that predatory birds cannot reach them. These farms now supply high-quality fish all year round to the Israeli market.

Here is another example of Israeli ingenuity focusing on a problem, and finding a solution that not only benefits its own population, but also offers expert technical advice and help to many countries worldwide.

Fish farming has taken off in the arid Negev region – one of the driest areas in the world.

Each year millions of fingerlings are put back to replenish the fish stock of Lake Kinneret.

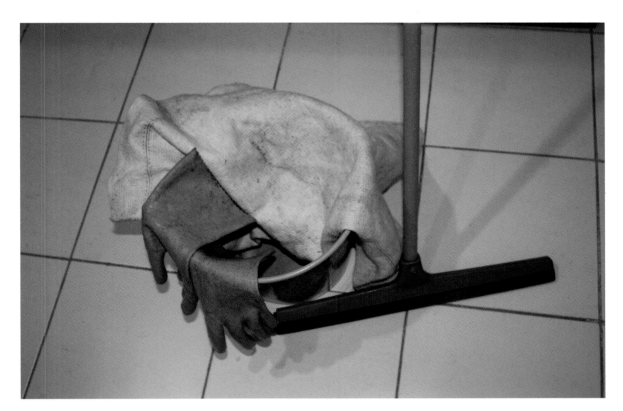

Floor Cleaning

The ubiquitous sponja

One of the most puzzling phenomena about this country is the messianic fervor with which Israelis regard their floor-cleaning equipment, namely the *sponja*.

After thirty years of trying, I still cannot master the art of getting it to clean the floors properly. Instead it is an exercise in total frustration.

Every Israeli you speak to swears that it is the only and the best way of cleaning the floor. "I will teach you" they say, beating their chests. "All you do is wrap the *smartut* [rag] around the *magav* [stick] and hey, presto."

What they fail to understand is that with every movement of the stick the rag falls off. Water is spread where it is not meant to be and the floor remains dirty. I am convinced that the *sponja* is designed by an association of subversive domestic workers wishing to maintain their monopoly on cleaning and deter any well-meaning householders ambitious enough to try to clean their own floors.

Israeli websites maintain this myth with a proliferation of advertisements for, among other things, "the most widely sold rag in the country" – just where do they get their statistics from? Have you ever answered a customer research project on rags?

And another promotes "the wonder floor cloth – a revolution in cleaning that comes with a one-year guarantee." Can anyone tell me how a floor cloth might fail to meet up to its guarantee?

Photo: Eyal Bartov. Courtesy of Yossi Leshem.

Flying with the Birds

Flying the glider with a flock of birds

Israel is a paradise for bird watchers, given its location on the migratory path between Europe, Africa and Asia, along which half a billion birds fly twice each year. However while wonderful for nature enthusiasts, it is a huge cause for concern for both military and commercial aviation.

A twenty-pound pelican that collides with an aircraft flying at six hundred miles per hour does so with a force of one hundred tons, and even a two-pound kite can hit a plane with an impact of fifteen tons.

Military aircraft flying at lower altitudes than commercial flights are at greater risk. Since 1972, sixty-six hundred bird strikes caused untold damage and loss of life to the Israel Air Force and more planes have been lost in this way than through enemy action.

In 1980 matters began to look up, literally, when a young ornithologist, Yossi Leshem, chose to study migratory birds for his doctoral thesis. He hired a motorized glider and a pilot and spent over fifteen hundred hours, sometimes eleven hours a day, tracking the birds' movements. He discovered that, whereas birds usually follow the same routes, the height at which they fly varies between 3,500 and 10,000 feet.

On the basis of his advice, the Israel Air Force changed their flight paths so that during the main

Bird-
related
damage
to aircraft
has fallen
by 76
percent.

Photo: Yossi Leshem

Yossi flying with the birds

migratory seasons their planes never fly below 6,000 feet except for takeoff and landing.

Yossi next established a project, with the support of Israel Aircraft Industries, launching aerial drones to photograph the birds from above. He purchased an old Russian radar system, originally designed to study metereological patterns but adapted in Israel to identify migration routes with more precision.

What he has in effect created is an extensive air traffic control system for birds and aircraft. He has also encouraged the recruitment of hundreds of bird watchers in the Palestinian territories and Israel, who regularly contact the Israel Air Force when they sight flocks of birds, specifying their location and approximate altitude.

In my travels with Alon he regularly stops the car to phone the IAF to report the location on some flock of birds or other.

As a result primarily of Yossi's findings, bird-related damage to aircraft has fallen by 76 percent and saved millions of dollars. This has been the catalyst for further studies, including a project

with the German government in which miniature transmitters are fixed to birds in order to track their flight habits.

Yossi also works closely with the Royal Jordanian Air Force and the Turkish Air force, and many western governments come to him for advice. He was instrumental in providing information on bird movements over Kuwait, Iraq and Saudi Arabia during the first Gulf War, thus helping to minimize casualties.

This man is one of those rare characters blessed with an abiding passion, in his case for birds, which has resulted in the development of strategies that not only protect his beloved avian friends but also contribute to the safety and wellbeing of mankind.

His enthusiasm and energy are unceasing. His latest ambition is to encourage all twenty-two nations from Mozambique to Turkey to declare the entire Rift Valley a World Heritage Site. This may sound like a tall order, but if anyone can do this, it will be Yossi Leshem, a giant of a man in every respect, bringing countries to levels of cooperation that politicians rarely achieve.

Folk Dancing

Dancing at Gordon Beach, Tel Aviv

Folk dancing can be traced back to the early pioneers who came to Israel in the 1920s – ex-urbanites infused with the ideal of working the land. Dance was a way of expressing joy in their new environment. The original songs referred to shepherds, camels and herds. These may no longer exist, but there still remains a core of songs expressing love for the countryside and everything that it embodies.

After 1948 and the establishment of the State of Israel, folk dancing was encouraged in the hope that it would become a major part of an "Israeli" culture, a means of absorbing immigrants who came from many different countries into one homogeneous group.

New dance steps have been created over the years and there has been a huge input of "Mizrachi" music from countries such as Bukharia, Yemen and Turkey, all of which have left their influence.

Devotees of folk dancing fear that in modern times it has little appeal for the young and that nobody under thirty is likely to take part. They need not worry. One thing is certain – the under-thirties will inevitably one day be the over-thirties, and besides, schools and youth groups include "*rikudei am*" (folk dancing) in their syllabus, even at primary school level.

Adult groups meet regularly throughout the country to dance together, some coming for the social aspect, others for their love of dance or exercise. Open-air sessions take place at the Tel Aviv seafront every Saturday morning when at least a hundred men and women of all ages and types dance enthusiastically for a couple of hours. A similar group in Jerusalem meets at the First Station every Sunday evening.

It is a complete joy and exhilarating to watch. They all seem to know the steps although no one leads the session or teaches the moves. I am longing to have a go. I guess I just have to watch, copy what the others do and jump in at the deep end.

It can become quite addictive. I have reliably been told that this is also the place to go if you want to meet a partner or find a lover. A possible forerunner of the internet dating service.

One strange phenomenon worth noting is the extent to which Israeli folk dance has been embraced worldwide. There are groups in South America, Canada, Australia, Taiwan and Japan and in at least thirty states in the USA.

Extraordinary that a dance style from such a small country as Israel has spread so widely. Perhaps it is supported by expatriate Israelis, wishing to keep in touch with their roots, but what is in it for non-Israelis? As Alice in Wonderland said: "Curiouser and curiouser!"

Sunday night session at the First Station, Jerusalem

Fossilized Trees

Fossilized tree trunks in the Negev, 5.6 feet high

Trees have figured significantly in my travels around Israel.

One incident to arouse my curiosity occurred in the area of the Ramon Crater in the Negev, when I noticed a sign that read "Ammonite Wall." On asking Alon, my guide, what kind of fossils there were in the area, he replied, "You want to see fossils? I'll show you fossils!" And so, after half an hour of driving over rocky sand dunes, we came across a cluster of what can only be described as massive petrified trees.

There they lay in a copse, each trunk measuring anything from between ten to sixteen feet in diameter. If I were standing next to one it would have been almost my height. It took me complete-

ly by surprise as I was expecting to see something small that I could hold in my hand – instead we were greeted by these immense tree trunks lying supinely on the sandy earth – majestic reminders of an age longer ago than one can comprehend.

I found it awe inspiring to reflect that this area, which is now a vast treeless desert, was at one time a dense forest, probably populated by a genus similar to the sequoia tree. Petrified trees are found at various locations in the United States but these are mostly in forested areas, whereas to come across them in an arid desert such as in Israel makes the find all the more dramatic.

Today almost two-thirds of Israel comprises desert, but it is the only desert in the world that is shrinking rather than growing. All of this is thanks to the efforts of the farmers and agriculturalists who are seeking to realize the dream of Israel's first prime minister, David Ben-Gurion – to see the desert bloom.

Large areas of parched earth have been brought back to life and as far south as Eilat it is now possible to see brilliant patches of emerald fields punctuating the ochre landscape.

The fruits, vegetables and other plants that flourish here are a testimony to the massive effort invested in research into crop development in arid conditions and the imaginative and innovative management of scarce water resources.

It is unrealistic to think that the desert might

Immense
tree trunks
lying
supinely on
the sandy
earth

one day revert to its original dense forests. But we have at least been privileged to see, in our own lifetime, this desert bloom – itself something of a small miracle.

The desert blooms

Photo: Alon Galili

Friendship

Old friends

Nothing can compare with those friendships that are formed when serving in the Israel Defense Forces (IDF). Military service is compulsory for both men and women. Call-up age is eighteen. Men serve three years, women two.

Since the establishment of the State of Israel there have been nine wars, so the likelihood of recruits seeing active duty is high. Many times have I been told stories by veteran Israelis who confirm that their closest friends are those with whom they served. There is nothing like being under fire to bring people close together.

One of the basic obligations of a soldier in the IDF – the concept of comradeship – extends to all ranks, from the highest officer to the newest recruit. A soldier is expected to risk his life for his fellow soldiers and not desert the wounded on the battlefield. This is a vital principle to instill complete trust among soldiers and strengthen their sense of mission and team spirit.

Once army service ends, soldiers continue to serve every couple of years on reserve duty (*miluim*). This reunites them with their friends, reinforcing the ties that they have. *Miluim* terminates at the age of forty, but some soldiers volunteer to continue serving much longer, especially in order to keep up contact with their buddies.

Some may complain of the disruption to their work and family life, but at the end of their month together there is much hugging and emotion when once again they bid each other good-bye. Hardened soldiers they may be, but there is a huge tender spot reserved for army friends and this deep-rooted respect and affection extends also to the widows and orphans of colleagues who died in service.

They may have little in common in everyday life, but the connection from being in uniform together is something quite unique – an intense relationship that lasts a lifetime.

An intense relationship that lasts a lifetime.

Another old friend

Expert practitioners can do this at enormous speed without thinking.

Garinim (Sunflower Seeds)

Meir from Afula, famed vendor of seeds

Every weekend before Shabbat, an Israeli male must ensure two things – one, that he has his newspaper, and two, that he has an ample supply of *garinim* to last until Sunday.

Garinim are sunflower seeds, and for the connoisseur it is imperative that they are bought freshly roasted, sold in brown paper bags of one hundred to two hundred grams. Not for him the cellophane-wrapped variety from a supermarket. Go to Garinim Afula – there you will meet Meir, an Iraqi Jew whose family has been selling these seeds for years. He is something of an institution, with customers coming from far and wide to buy from him.

The technique of eating them is something that only a native-born Israeli can master. As he demonstrated, the seeds are cracked between the teeth, the kernel is eaten and the husks are unceremoniously spat out. Experienced practitioners can do this at enormous speed without thinking, certainly without stopping and usually without taking their eyes off the pages of a newspaper. I am reliably informed that really top experts can also hold a conversation at the same time. The practice is totally addictive. Any dish of *garinim* has to be finished, however full it may be.

Why there is no category for this in the Guinness Book of Records escapes me. It certainly warrants inclusion, and it must surely be an Israeli who would achieve the world record.

For the bystander this national pastime is not without its downside. You may not mind the constant sound of nuts being cracked between your neighbor's teeth, on the bus for example, but you will object to the salvo of husks that inevitably fly in your direction. A visit to some public events, particularly football matches, ends in an ankle-deep trudge through piles of discarded shells.

What a fascinating sociological phenomenon, one which I liken to the practice of eating an artichoke – a great deal of effort and flourish with not much to show for it in the end.

Khaled at Bahari, the best garinim *place in Jerusalem, established 53 years ago and still going strong.*

Goats

Tariq minding his herd

I have often pondered how strange it is that we allocate specific characteristics to certain animals. Sheep are supposedly amiable but a bit stupid. Goats on the other hand have had a raw deal as nothing very positive is ever said about them.

They were one of the earliest animals to be domesticated in the time of Cain and Abel – Abel being a herdsman. Stories about shepherds and goatherds abound in the Bible.

It seems that goats have always had a bad reputation, partially because of their association through Christianity with Satan, but most likely because of their antisocial grazing habits. Unlike sheep, they will eat just about anything, crop very close to the ground and demolish bushes and low-growing plants. They even climb trees, denuding them of their foliage and fruit.

This characteristic was well observed by the early rabbis, who issued strict injunctions as to where goats may and may not graze. Failure to follow this resulted in later years, particularly after the Muslim conquest, in damaging the natural environment, from which it has taken centuries to recover.

This ruling protecting the environment persists until today in Israel, but notwithstanding, Bedouin farmers flourish in the Negev with their herds and there is an established industry of goat farms producing superlative cheeses, considered by nutritionists as a healthier alternative to that of cows' milk.

The truth of the matter is that goats are both intelligent and extremely curious animals. The billy goat demonstrates admirable single-mindedness and leadership qualities, suitable for any of our politicians, rather than being a follower like his sheepish cousins. Perhaps it was these forthright traits that people were none too happy about. After all no one really likes egoistic, strong-minded individuals.

The goat has, therefore, been consigned to the bottom of the popularity pile. A fact reinforced in contemporary parlance, where we find copious references to this much-maligned animal. "An old goat" signifies an elderly lecher, and "to act the goat" – is to fool around.

However, in the world of comedy goats have been recognized for their intellect:

One day a rabbi mislaid his precious Bible. Two weeks later a goat came up to him carrying the Bible in its mouth. The rabbi could not believe his eyes. He took the book out of the goat's mouth, looked heavenward and exclaimed, "It's a miracle!"

"Not really" said the goat. "Your name is written on the inside cover."

Goats denuding tree branches

Courtesy of Zichron Menachem

Hair Donation

Children waiting to have their hair cut

"I had a very emotional week," said Revital, my friend from Tel Aviv. Her teenage daughter had decided to have her beautiful hair cut off in order to give it to a charity that creates wigs for small children suffering from hair loss through chemotherapy.

A nationwide campaign had been launched in Israel encouraging those with long hair to donate it. My friend described the mixed emotions she felt as she cut off her daughter's crowning glory and watched it tumble to the floor with each snip of the scissors. She felt a mixture of pride that her fifteen-year-old child would do this, together with

pangs of regret as her daughter was shorn of the locks she had treasured for so long.

Richard Titmuss, the pioneering social researcher, wrote a seminal book on the altruism of blood donation in Britain, entitled *The Gift Relationship*. The donation of hair comes into this same category. A girl's hair is her pride and joy, and to relinquish it for the benefit of others is an act of supreme generosity toward an unknown recipient. In Jewish thought it is said that the best form of charity is to give it anonymously.

Zichron Menachem, based in Jerusalem, was established to support families affected by cancer. They focus on children, who are particularly badly hit when they lose their eyebrows and hair, as they can become objects of curiosity or ridicule. To receive a wig, matching as closely as possible to their original hair, boosts self-confidence and helps them to fight the cancer more positively. To quote fourteen-year-old Efrat: "When I wear my wig, I feel like I'm taking a vacation from the cancer."

Religious sensitivities are also catered for. The Kaplan Medical Center appealed for hair to be used to create side curls (*pei'ot*) for religious young men. This might sound trivial to some, but imagine the thoughts of a boy who all his life has worn side curls, suddenly to lose them and immediately look different from his peers. Having them replaced is one small way of making him feel less noticeable and less conscious of his cancer.

In 2011 Zichron Menachem organized a national hair drive in Israel. Hairdressing salons throughout the country offered to cut hair for free and famous personalities became involved, visiting sick children in hospitals.

The event marking the end of the campaign had a border police unit ascend the Aviv Tower – the tallest building in Israel – and rappel from the top using a seven-thousand-foot-long braid made of hair collected from fifteen hundred donors.

Courtesy of Zichron Menachem

A donor waits her turn

"When I wear my wig, I feel like I'm taking a vacation from cancer."

Perhaps this was just an updated version of Grimm's fairy tale about Rapunzel who, locked in a tower, let down her tresses to enable the hero to climb up and effect a rescue. I suppose that what they did in Tel Aviv was not rappelling but rapunzelling?

Whatever you choose to call it, this initiative to collect hair for children suffering the effects of chemotherapy is yet another example of the caring society that is Israel.

Hassadna: Music for Life

Avraham – now a star pupil

In 2006 Lena Nemirovsky was appointed as director of the Hassadna Music School in Jerusalem and decided to establish a new project, to offer disadvantaged children the chance to experience music at the highest level. Scholarship places were offered to Ethiopian children, referred from the local Battered Women's Home. They were from some of the poorest families, in which drug abuse and violence was common and parents had to work long hours for minimal pay. Their children, with no extracurricular activities, were unsupervised and spent most of their time on the streets.

The authorities told Lena she was wasting her time. Undeterred, she and her colleagues embarked on lengthy discussions with the parents to get them involved. The course began. Day one the children came. Day two they arrived late. Day three they turned up but forgot their music and finally they didn't come at all.

Lena realized that the school must interact with the families at a much deeper level. Older music students acting as mentors now visit the children at home to help them practice. Each child is provided with a piano, violin or other instrument, which is kept at home. Transport to lessons, food and clothing are supplied, as well as lots of encouragement. The families eventually realized the huge benefits that music can bring to their children and the tremendous boost in self-confidence that it generates.

After six hard years Lena is seeing the fruits of her labor. A year ago an Ethiopian father came to the school to ask if they would accept his child. This was a hugely significant turning point and today there is a long waiting list.

Children with severe physical or mental conditions are also offered places. One child plays piano with only one finger so special musical arrangements are written for him. An autistic child has minimal attention span – whatever the problem, the school and in particular the other pupils respond with positive support.

On arrival each child becomes part of a group – a member of a "musical family." Confidence grows, as does self-esteem which translates rapidly into other areas of life, particularly schooling. Bullying, a common problem in most schools, is unheard of at Hassadna. All students support whoever needs help, taking pride in each other's achievements – a rare gift, for both recipient and giver.

The impact on their lives is dramatic and deeply moving. Jacob, blind with severe physical disabilities and distorted hands, plays the piano for hours and his joy is evident. His teacher said, "One day, in the depths of winter, Jacob suddenly shouted, 'This is sunlight!' He was playing on the top register and his music shimmered and sparkled. The beauty of the moment was miraculous."

Rasha, a blind orphan Arab girl with severe autism, was abandoned by her parents and raised in an orphanage. Her love of music was identified and she came to the academy twenty-two years ago. She is taught by a religious Jewish woman, and the bond between them is magical. Without music Rasha's life would be meaningless. With it, her whole being lights up.

I attended a concert given by some of these young musicians. Their faces shone with pleasure at our applause. Their enjoyment was palpable. Music has opened doors for them and enriched their lives immeasurably. In March 2014 their wind ensemble performed at Carnegie Hall in New York – an outstanding achievement that met with a rapturous reception from the audience.

Hassadna's work is life enhancing and inspirational. I shall watch with pleasure to see these children develop, for the gift they have received will stand them in good stead all their lives.

Loving the violin

Heritage Restored

Andalusian garden

Having lived in Jerusalem for twenty-eight years it always comes as a surprise to find something unexpected in this city. One such discovery was the North African Heritage Center, barely a five-minute walk from our home.

Hidden away behind the Waldorf Astoria, and fronted by a tiled and flower-filled Andalusian garden, lies the David Amar World Center for North African Jewish Heritage.

It opened to the public in 2012 to promote and reflect the rich history of North African Judaism. The center is housed in a stunning four-story building with a central courtyard that sweeps up to a decorative glass dome at the top of the building and through which shafts of light illuminate the exquisitely carved massive cedar beams, imported from the Atlas mountains, and the perfectly formed arches of traditional Moorish architecture.

Looking upward one's eyes feast on a confection of delicate filigree tracery, hand-carved from pure white alabaster. The floors on each level are ablaze with the variegated colors of handmade tiles copied from traditional designs that have survived over the centuries. The aesthetic cohesion of the building extends even to the interiors of the elevators and bathrooms.

To achieve this level of perfection, twenty-four expert craftsmen were brought from Morocco. These artisans began training as youngsters to learn the unique skill, handed down from father to son, called "Zellige," following age-old methods and a strictly observed code of surface decoration.

The technique adopts mathematical principles of design. The star pattern can incorporate from twelve to one hundred points, each element meticulously measured. Terra-cotta tiles are coated

Carved alabaster and archway decorations

Shafts
of light
illuminate
the
exquisitely
carved
massive
cedar beams.

with a plaster surface, into which colored enamel chips are carefully embedded to create complex interconnecting designs.

Other patterns represent honeycombs, steps, webs and checkerboards. The Dutch painter M.C. Escher (1898–1972) adapted these principles as a source of inspiration for his own work, particularly after visiting the Alhambra in Granada.

The area where the center is located was established in the mid-nineteenth century by Rabbi David Ben Shimon, the son of a well-to-do merchant from Rabat in Morocco. He arrived in

Jerusalem at age twenty-eight and set about creating a Mughrabi community in what was previously unoccupied wasteland, and which subsequently became known as Mahane Yisrael. His magnificent building comprised a school (Talmud Torah), a meeting room and a synagogue set beside an open square, on the perimeter of which small dwellings were erected.

At that time almost all the Moroccan Jews in Jerusalem lived in poverty within the walls of the Old City. Ben Shimon encouraged them to join him to live and work in Mahane Yisrael, much as Sir Moses Montefiore had done for Ashkenazi Jews at Mishkenot Sha'ananim.

Ben Shimon was not only charismatic and learned, but also highly conscientious in caring for his growing number of followers, providing anyone in need with food and basic necessities. To enable this he sent emissaries to Jewish communities in Islamic countries to raise funds, keeping scrupulously detailed accounts of every penny spent. Such was his reputation that many outside his community were drawn to study with him. Sadly he did not live to enjoy old age, dying in his forties. He was buried on the Mount of Olives.

After the War of Independence the area became a no-man's-land, within range of Jordanian snipers in the Old City. The building was looted and fell into disrepair. It was partially restored after 1967 and again in the late 1980s. The initiative to restore the present building, with an additional floor, came fairly recently. It was dedicated to David Amar, a wealthy Moroccan businessman who was financial adviser to King Hassan II, the father of Muhammad VI, the present king of Morocco.

The building houses a museum, archives, a library and research center and exhibition areas. A dynamic program of activities focuses on different aspects of Jewish life, of which music is an essential theme. Sessions are held in ethnic music, liturgical texts (*piyutim*) and special sessions to revive the "lingua franca" of Moroccan Jewry – a unique variation of Judeo-Arabic being another "Jewish language" much as Yiddish in the Ashkenazi world and Ladino for the Sephardim.

When the Moroccans came penniless to Israel in the early 1950s they had a very difficult time, as they were looked down upon by Ashkenazi Jews. They were called *Marocaim Sakinim* (knife wielders) and felt like second-class citizens. This attitude and resentment still prevails in some quarters even today.

This center is invaluable not only for educating Israelis and tourists about an important part of our Jewish world, but also for restoring a justifiable pride to Moroccan Jews in their rich heritage dating back to Greco-Roman times.

While visiting the center, I joined a tour group of elderly Moroccan women. On entering its small synagogue they burst into spontaneous song – it was deeply moving and an evident expression of pure joy in rediscovering their lost heritage.

Some told me that even though they had arrived in Israel as children, while visiting the center they found that their deepest memories were stirred, recalling places, sights and sounds from very early childhood. This place is a gift to be cherished and handed down to future generations to ensure that their history will never be forgotten.

Zellige tile decoration

Slowly it creaked into action and, unseen by the enemy, made its way across to the other side.

A Hidden Lifeline

Avshalom's Way cable car

It is December 1947. Two young soldiers stand looking out of the window toward the Old City of Jerusalem, from their outpost at St John's Eye Hospital. They are waiting for dusk to fall.

The place they occupy is the operations room for the newly designed cable car called Avshalom's Way, which it is hoped will bring help to their besieged compatriots stranded in the Old City only two hundred yards away across a deep valley.

The Jews living there were under attack by the forces of the Jordanian Arab Legion led by its British commander Glubb Pasha, who had superior weaponry and strength of numbers compared to the ill-armed and tiny group of Jews battling for survival. Conditions were appalling and they had

resorted to eating mallow leaves to obtain basic vitamins. Nothing could get through to them, neither food, nor medical aid nor equipment.

This new cable car was their only hope. To call it such was something of a misnomer; it was more like a metal coffin – a simple oblong box that could carry a maximum load of 550 pounds. The "lift" had been loaded up with basic essential supplies and weapons and it was just a question of waiting for dark to fall so that it could be sent over to Mount Zion.

It could only operate at night. During the day it was lowered to the ground and hidden in undergrowth so that it would invisible to the Jordanian forces. The lift was operated by two soldiers – they

Today
a small
museum
devoted
to the
cable car
is located
in the
Mount Zion
Hotel in
Jerusalem.

Cable car waiting to cross the valley

grasped the handles that worked the machine and began to winch it across the valley. Slowly it creaked into action and, unseen by the enemy, made its way across to the other side, the journey taking two minutes.

On arrival it was emptied and reloaded, this time with an injured soldier who was carefully lowered onto a stretcher and placed in the box. Medical personnel and transport were waiting for him on the other side to rush him to hospital.

It is easy to imagine the tension, particularly when they were transferring the sick and injured, and the relief when their precious cargo reached relative safety.

How many times it crossed the valley each night is not recorded, but it operated regularly for six months until the armistice in July 1948. The cable car was then hidden, but maintained should it ever be needed again. It only became public knowledge in 1973 when its inventor Uriel Hefez was awarded the Israel Security Prize. He was an outstanding and courageous soldier who rescued

wounded while under fire. He was also involved in the efforts to save schoolchildren from a terrorist attack on a school bus in Ma'alot in 1974, during which action he was seriously wounded.

Today a small museum devoted to the cable car is located in the Mount Zion Hotel in Jerusalem.

I visit there often. For me it has a profound and palpable sense of history. I rarely see anyone else and to stand alone in the room where such significant historic events took place is deeply moving. For me it evokes the spirit of those heroic times and brings into sharp focus the atmosphere and drama of what happened more than sixty-five years ago.

Honey with a Sting in the Tale?

Beehives on the roof of Fortnum & Mason

According to the Bible, God spoke to Moses at the burning bush, promising to bring the Children of Israel to a "good and spacious land, flowing with milk and honey."

Honey is mentioned in the Bible about twenty times, but rabbinical sources maintain that these refer to syrup from dates or figs, not to honey from bees.

This view was called into question in 2007 when archaeologists excavated the Iron Age town of Tel Rehov in the Jordan Valley. They unearthed a number of clay cylinders, identified as beehives on the basis of evidence from ancient Egyptian wall paintings.

They concluded that these cylinders were the remains of a large apiary dating back three thousand years and that an estimated two hundred hives would have housed more than one million bees, indicating that this was a highly sophisticated industry.

Each hive measured thirty inches long by sixteen inches in diameter, with a flap on one side to allow bees to enter and a lid on the other side to access the honeycomb. The cylinders were stacked on top of each other, as seen in the sketch overleaf.

Surprisingly, the remains of bees found in the hives revealed that they originated in Turkey. Professor Amihai Mazar, of the Hebrew University,

Ancient Egyptian wall painting

said, "This is a very special discovery as we had no previous evidence of bringing creatures from such a distance, especially bees, which represents a complicated and sophisticated type of agriculture."

It suggests that extensive trading in commodities existed at the time and this trade in bees may well have been one of the first examples of an Israeli "start-up" company.

Honeybees have always been essential to mankind. In ancient times honey was used as a medicine and for sweetening food, while beeswax was valued as a sealant, a lubricant and for making candles. But more crucial is the role that honeybees play in nature. It is estimated that they are responsible for 25 percent of the world's pollination, providing vital sources of food. Without the bees' sterling activities, our food supplies would be sadly depleted.

This vision of an ominous future was brought to our attention recently because of the disappearance of many bee colonies throughout the world as a result of Colony Collapse Disorder (CCD). In the United States 80 percent of bees have been lost in this way. Little is known for certain about the causes of CCD. It may be a parasite, a virus or the excessive use of certain pesticides.

In Israel, Professor Ilan Sela of the Hebrew University discovered the IAPV virus, which is linked to CCD. The treatment he developed, together with a US company, has rehabilitated up to 70 percent of the hives on which it was tested. Israeli scientists also developed special strains of eucalyptus and acacia trees that produce blossoms several times a year, so as to maintain a steady nectar supply for the bees.

Attention is also being focused on pesticides in common use, as these have proven to inhibit bees when they forage for food. Normally bees from a single hive can cover up to forty square miles of territory checking on the availability of nectar. They then return and perform a "waggle dance" for the other bees in the hive – their means of passing on information regarding the location of nectar. An extraordinary sight to see.

A fascination with bees is shared by a growing number of devotees, perhaps prompted by this world crisis. Steve Benbow is one such character. He has been passionately interested in insect life since childhood and as an adult, and with no experience, built his own hive on a London rooftop ten years ago. Today he is responsible for hives on the roofs of some of London's most prestigious buildings such as Harrods, both Tate Galleries and the National Gallery. At Fortnum and Mason, that elegant emporium of food and fashion, Steve cares for four beehives, in this case architect designed, using their well-known house colors of

Courtesy of Fortnum & Mason

Bees returning to the hive.

Lebanon, then controlled by Vichy France, to prevent Nazi Germany from gaining a stronghold in the north.

Alon remembers Anzac troops coming to the kibbutz at night to give them weapons captured from the French. The Anzacs felt a special kinship with the kibbutz as they too were mostly farmers. Alon found it somewhat confusing that while part of the British army was friendly, others, such as the military police, would frequently descend on the kibbutz and create havoc, turning everything upside down in their search for arms.

The kibbutzniks came up with a novel hiding place, digging holes beneath the beehives where they secreted the guns. When the military police came to investigate, a member of the kibbutz would pull a wire attached to the hive. The flap opened and the bees swarmed. Needless to say the MPs beat a hasty retreat.

An early example of Israelis thinking outside the box?

green and gold. It is possible now to visit these hives, perhaps a rather unusual take on "shopping in London."

Back in Israel bees served another essential role, in a tale known only to a few – one of whom is my traveling companion Alon, who grew up on Kibbutz Dan near the border with Lebanon. At that time the British authorities governed Palestine. In 1941 the Allied army invaded Syria and

One of
the first
examples
of an Israeli
"start-up"
company.

Courtesy of Alon Galili

Into the Wild: Conservation

Nubian Ibex

Over the years many species of wildlife that once lived in the Middle East have become extinct due to urban and industrial development, the destruction of their natural habitat and hunting.

At the turn of the nineteenth century, with the advent of automatic weapons, three animals in particular were eradicated from desert areas: the onager, the ostrich and the Arabian or white oryx.

In the 1960s, thanks to dedicated visionaries, the Hai Bar Nature Reserve was established in Israel. Its main objective was to breed those animals mentioned in the Bible that were no longer extant and reintroduce them to the wild.

To date they have succeeded in repopulating the onager and the white oryx (*re'em*). Their experience with ostriches was not quite so successful. A large number were bred, but upon being released the birds ran two miles toward Jordan. They had to be rounded up and brought back as it was feared that Jordanian hunters might kill them. On the next attempt to release them, the ostriches changed direction but this time ran south toward

Sinai and Egypt. Again they had to be rounded up and brought back to the reserve. Here they reside, until it is decided how and where to release them.

Hai Bar have a second center in the north of Israel at Carmel, where they have managed to increase the numbers of roe deer, fallow deer, Egyptian vultures and the fish eagle.

In addition to repopulating biblical species, Hai Bar has a successful program of breeding endangered species that are not necessarily indigenous to Israel, such as the scimitar oryx and the addax. Both of these once roamed the Sahara, but over the years were hunted to extinction. In 1999 eight scimitar-horned oryx were returned to Senegal where they now survive; their numbers have increased and they are regarded as the country's national animal.

In 2010 Israel passed a law prohibiting hunting for sport – legislation that is enforced with heavy fines for transgressors. Hunting is permitted only when animals are a threat to people, or to prevent ecological damage.

This legislation, together with the continued efforts of organizations such as Hai Bar, represents an oasis of hope in a world where, sadly, so many species have a grim future and will inevitably be consigned to the picture books of history.

Their experience with ostriches was not quite so successful.

Ostriches on the move

Courtesy of Doron Nissim

The Jerusalem–Jaffa Railway Line

The railway line today, 2015

In 1892 the first Near Eastern rail link was completed between the port of Jaffa on the Mediterranean and Jerusalem.

Discussions about building a railway began in 1838, involving Sir Moses Montefiore, Lord Palmerston, the British prime minister and the grand vizier of Turkey Ali Pasha. Then followed fifty years of political arguing between European governments, but it was only after the involvement of Joseph Navon, an entrepreneur from Jerusalem, that the project became a reality.

As an Ottoman subject, despite his many influential contacts he struggled to raise money from Jews in Europe. Eventually the railway was built by a French company and Navon was awarded the French Légion d'Honneur, plus the title of *bey* (lord) from the Turks for his endeavors.

Theodore Herzl, the Zionist leader, was not impressed by this rickety, narrow, three-feet gauge railway. He complained, among other things, of the lack of ashtrays and wrote that "it was a wretched little line from Jaffa to Jerusalem which was of course quite inadequate for our needs" (Paul Cotterell, *The Railways of Palestine and Israel* [Abingdon: Tourret, 1984], 10).

Construction was an international affair with engineers from Poland, Italy, Austria and Switzerland and workers from Egypt, Sudan and Algiers,

Colville's 1933 plates

"It was a
wretched
little line
from
Jaffa to
Jerusalem"

as well as local Arabs. They suffered a heavy death toll while breaking through rocks to create cuttings and build bridges. Most bridges were stone, but others were designed and built with iron supplied by the Eiffel Company of France. Additional problems were encountered while importing heavy equipment, as the jetty at Jaffa was flimsy and on one occasion was swept away by a heavy storm.

Nevertheless, the first passenger journey took place in August 1892. It took four hours, less than traveling by horse and carriage, and as the train struggled uphill, passengers could get out, pick flowers and rejoin the train at a later stage.

Today two and a half miles of this track has been transformed into a landscaped walkway in Jerusalem. The rails from a later period remain, still fixed to the steel sleepers (ties), each imprinted with the name Colvilles and the date – 1933.

I walk there often and feel a strong sense of history, so I was intrigued to find out more. According to Grace's *Guide of British Industrial History*, David Colville and Sons was founded in Motherwell, near Glasgow, in 1871. Originally producers of malleable iron, they switched to steel production in 1880, becoming a massive conglomerate that was eventually absorbed into British Steel in 1967.

I cannot even begin to understand the logistics of transporting thousands of heavy plates from Scotland to Palestine. It was a massive undertaking. British Mandate authorities widened the track during WW1 from the Turkish Hejaz gauge of 1.05 meters (3.4 feet) to the standard 1.43 meters (4.69 feet) and it was in 1933 that Colvilles became involved, replacing the old wooden sleepers with the metal ones we still see today imprinted with their name.

Recently I noticed that on one side of the track the sleepers have now been covered by sand and grass. I hope the rest remain visible, as a silent witness to those who came to Jerusalem so many years ago to build a railway line that still exists for us to enjoy.

Today, particularly after the First Station area was opened as an entertainment center, the railway line is used by many families, cyclists, joggers and others taking the opportunity to stroll and enjoy the environment. I guess the original founders would be delighted to know it still exists, albeit in a different form.

Joseph Bau House

Clila Bau sitting at her father's desk which, serendipitously, he recovered from the ghetto after the war. It now has pride of place in the museum.

In my travels to seek lesser-known facts and places, I came across a story that moved me so deeply that it was difficult to put out of my mind.

Hidden in a small street in Tel Aviv is the Joseph Bau House. Not a single one of my friends knew about it, yet Joseph was a unique individual who survived the worst of times and managed to bring a beacon of light to others through his optimism, talent and wit.

Born 1920 in Krakow, Poland, Joseph showed great artistic promise and was accepted at the Academy of Fine Arts, Krakow, where his studies included graphics and Gothic lettering. Little did

he realize how these skills would guarantee his future.

His studies were interrupted when he was forced into the Krakow ghetto. The Nazis, learning of his talents, coerced him to draw all their signage and maps. But Joseph was also blessed with the ability to bring joy to others. Jews would crowd into his small room to hear him play the mandolin and read his poetry. He lit up their lives, providing a brief respite from the desolation of ghetto life. While there, he began forging documents for the Jewish underground. Thanks to him, many Jews managed to escape to safety.

In 1943 he was transferred to the Plaszow death camp. By day he worked for the Nazis, but in secret he continued to forge documents to help Jewish prisoners. When asked why he had never tried to escape, he replied, "If I had left, who would have remained to help them?"

He said he never regretted being taken to the camp, for it was there that he fell in love with Rebecca Tannenbaum, who became his wife. Their romance reads like a movie script. Dressed as a woman, he risked death by smuggling himself into the women's camp. His mother, also an inmate, performed a "marriage" ceremony. This featured in the Spielberg film *Schindler's List*.

That same night two men were caught and shot for entering the women's camp. Joseph survived by lying across a bunk covered in rags. Women lay across him pretending to be asleep and he was not discovered. He then had to leap over an electric fence to return to the men's section in time for roll call. Miraculously, he survived.

His father and brother, not so fortunate, were murdered in the camp. In 1944, thanks to Rebecca's contacts, Joseph was placed on "Schindler's List" instead of her and transferred to a factory in Czechoslovakia, where he remained until the end of the war. Rebecca was sent to Auschwitz but survived by talking her way out of going to the gas chambers on three occasions.

Commemorative poster for posthumous wedding anniversary of Joseph and Rebecca Bau, 2014

Joseph told his daughters:

Two weeks after we arrived, Oskar Schindler called me and handed me my personal possessions which he had recovered from the camp. Among them was a diary and poems written during 1943–44. I was a total stranger, yet Schindler saved this diary and presented it to me. What kind of man would do this?

Rebecca and Joseph immigrated to Israel in 1950. He opened a studio in Tel Aviv where he created graphics, being the first person in Israel to work on cartoon films. He later made short films and commercials for television and became known as the Israeli Walt Disney. He also drew the titles for many Israeli movies.

In the Joseph Bau House you can see his movie screen, projection room and dark room. He built everything from scratch using anything available – a sewing machine engine and x-ray equipment parts.

Unbeknown to his family he worked for many years for the Mossad, Israel's secret service, forging documents for notable spies including Eli

יוסף באו

הרואה אין לו עיניים, המקשיב אין לו אוזניים והמדבר אין לו פה

*'The International Media', etching
by Joseph Bau, Bau Museum*

JOSEPH BAU

יוסף באו·

*'Arrow to Heart', etching
by Joseph Bau, Bau Museum.*

Cohen. Joseph's family had absolutely no idea that he was engaged in this work until after he died.

His daughters Clila and Hadasa keep his memory alive through traveling exhibitions and performances in Israel and abroad. The walls of the Bau House are covered with Joseph's artwork and the twelve books he wrote and illustrated, including *Dear God, Have You Ever Gone Hungry?* which has been translated into English, Polish, Spanish and Chinese. A second Chinese edition was published in 2015.

Joseph's works demonstrate the creativity, humor and optimism of an extraordinary talent.

Today there is a grave risk that this remarkable archive may have to close. This should not be allowed to happen. It is a dramatic testimony to a man who saved hundreds of Jewish lives, was the father of animation in Israel and a great writer, humorist and artist. His contribution to the culture of the country is of inestimable value, not the least being his unacknowledged work over so many years for the Mossad.

The Joy of Sax

My father with his band

I love the town of Jaffa. It is a fascinating blend of old and new. While modern cafés and stores have opened, there are still sufficient traditional artisans to ensure that it retains its unique character. A jewelry boutique sits alongside a workshop where a steel cutter plies his trade. A carpenter is located beside a contemporary ceramics gallery. A chandler is near a specialist coffee shop and a shoemaker close to a bespoke perfume store. At the heart of everything is the flea market. Goods of every description are piled up on the ground, offered by Arab and Jewish vendors who wait for enthusiastic collectors seeking a bargain.

Jaffa's reputation as a seaport, in fact the leading seaport in the Mediterranean between Alex-andria in Egypt and Tyre in Lebanon, goes back to biblical days. But its industrial activity began in the early nineteenth century when it was famed for its soap manufacture. However around 1870 modern industries such as metalwork, building materials and horse-drawn carriages were introduced into Palestine by the German Templars. Twenty years later Leon Stein, a Jewish pioneer from Poland, set up his metalwork factory, the largest and most advanced of its time, employing over 150 workers. Everything new from overseas arrived in Jaffa, whereas sleepy Jerusalem remained enveloped in its dusty blanket of religion and history.

In the early 1900s the production of orange

"Find any man who would give away part of himself for the book of another."

Ran repairing a sax

crates, barrels, cork, leather, olive oil and cosmetics began, as well as foodstuffs such as wine, ice, candy and noodles. Ink was a particularly important commodity, as most books and newspapers in the country were printed and published in Jaffa.

In 1911 the writer Shai Agnon, then twenty-five years old, worked in Jaffa on his first book, *And the Crooked Shall Be Made Straight*. He toiled without rest for days, feeding on bread and olives, reluctant to interrupt his creative flow. When the novella was finished he sent it to his good friend, the writer Y.H. Brenner, for an opinion. Brenner was captivated by the story and gathered a group of intellectuals to read and discuss it. Everyone wanted to be a part of the project. It was eventually agreed that the newspaper *Hapoel Hatzair* would print the first version.

Brenner kept the printing plates and next arranged to have the text published in book form by Jaffa publisher Aharon Itin. At one point, Itin demanded more money, which was not available. Brenner asked Agnon to meet him near the Jaffa Gate in Jerusalem. Together they walked toward a store, where Brenner entered and handed the storekeeper the suspenders (or *shlakers* in Yiddish) that he had recently bought. The trader gave him a refund and it was this money that enabled the publication to proceed. Brenner went back to wearing his old tattered belt. Agnon commented

at the time, "I ask you to find any man who would give away part of himself for the book of another."

During my explorations of Jaffa by far the most exciting find for me was the workshop where Ran Altitzer, a craftsman, was repairing wind instruments. I found this utterly fascinating since my Dad, Victor Daniels, had been an accomplished jazz musician who played saxophone and clarinet with some of the famous English big bands in the 1930s such as Billy Cotton, the most popular band leader of the day. When I was a child Dad would let me hold his musical instruments as I tried to get a sound out of them. Of course, as they were reed instruments, despite a lot of huffing and puffing on my part I could not even raise a "toot."

My father's two brothers were also professional musicians. After a career as a wrestler and then a teacher of unarmed combat in the Royal Air Force, Bert became one of the best session bass players in Britain, performing with Johnny Dankworth, at Abbey Studios, Ronnie Scott's and elsewhere. I remember a photo of him in his early days, posing and flexing his rippling muscles. My mother told me that he was so strong that two women could stand on his chest wearing high heels. For years I wondered why on earth anyone should want to do something so strange. I never did find out.

Uncle Ivor was an artillery gunner during the war and, despite suffering shell shock, became a talented guitarist, eventually winning the Melody Maker Guitarist of the Year award.

Back to Jaffa – Ran's father came from Switzerland in 1948 to fight for the young State of Israel. He did not play music, but lived and breathed it. Ran remembers being taken by his father regularly to hear the Israel Philharmonic Orchestra (IPO) and at nine years old he was, as he puts it, "forced" into playing the clarinet.

When he was twenty-one he decided to teach himself to play the flute. He practiced scales for up to eight hours a day until eventually his father, fed up with listening to him day in and day out, offered to find him a proper teacher – a flautist from the IPO. The first thing the teacher did was to insist that Ran hand over all his sheets of music. He said, "Now, you have to unlearn everything you taught yourself," and so Ran began again from scratch, playing children's songs. Happily, the teacher returned the music to Ran once he felt that his pupil was playing well enough.

Ran would often go to jam sessions on Jaffa beach with other music enthusiasts. One day one of the pads on his flute broke and he decided to try to repair it himself. Needless to say, he made a real mess of it. A friend of his father recommend-

ed that he go to the United States, where there was a renowned musical instrument repair factory that gave tuition. His father agreed to pay for the trip and, after eighteen months, Ran returned to Israel in 1983 and set up his own workshop.

He has had a varied career, but, as he says, "This is what I know and do best."

Ran is somewhat dismissive of his achievements but is a true artist. He practices for two hours a day and attends festivals where he enjoys playing Turkish music on his clarinet. He says that if he does not play music every day something important is missing in his life. Whether he admits it or not, he is a man of dedication and undoubted commitment to his art and is disciplined and rigorous in his work.

This, he claims, is inherited from his father, and Ran certainly fits the bill in terms of Swiss characteristics, including being a little reserved with strangers. I did not ask him if he has a penchant for cheese and chocolate.

Meeting Ran was a high spot of my Jaffa visit, but I suppose that, given my family history, there was simply no choice as to whether or not I would write this story. I am doing it for my dad – I know he would have enjoyed it.

He was so strong that two women could stand on his chest wearing high heels.

The three-ton hopper

David Ben-Gurion was refused membership for "unreliability."

Keeping the Secret

For the past seventeen years I have paid annual visits to Kibbutz Kfar Giladi in the far north of Israel but not once was I ever told about the fascinating history of the area. What a revelation it turned out to be.

It was here that Hashomer was started by a group of twelve idealists from Eastern Europe, who arrived in Ottoman Palestine in 1907 with the aim of working the land and setting up an organization to protect Jewish settlements from their hostile Arab neighbors.

Hashomer laid down strict rules for new members. They had to undergo a one-year trial period to demonstrate their commitment and bravery and prove their competence in handling

weapons, as well as their ability to keep secrets. The latter was vital during the Ottoman period since Hashomer's activities were clandestine. Not everyone was accepted. David Ben-Gurion was refused membership for "unreliability." The story goes that on one occasion he went missing from the kibbutz although his horse returned to the stables. Hashomer members went out looking for Ben-Gurion and found him reading under a tree.

Once a newcomer was admitted, an initiation ceremony was held in a cave at Sejera. Allegiance was sworn over a Bible and a revolver. This ceremony as well as other Hashomer traditions were adopted by the IDF and continue until today.

This need for secrecy led to the establishment

The hidden entrance to the slik*, looking down*

of hidden arms caches (*slik*s) throughout the country. I had never heard of them so when my guide, Torah, offered to show me one I could not refuse. We entered what resembled an old tool store. In the center was a large wheat hopper surrounded by sacks of grain.

She moved toward the hopper holding a massive spanner, turned something and, like magic, this three-ton piece of engineering moved silently to one side, revealing a hole in the floor less than three feet square. It was like a scene from an Indiana Jones movie. I was invited to climb down a steep vertical ladder into a black hole. Apprehensively, I made my way carefully, not knowing what awaited me.

At the bottom I was blown away – perhaps the wrong phrase considering that I was now in an ammunition store. Around me were shelves stocked with hundreds of boxes of bullets, rifles, machine guns and other weapons dating back many years, all perfectly maintained should they be needed again. This *slik*, established during the Ottoman period, was operating during the British Mandate when many of these weapons were "borrowed" from His Majesty's Government.

An engineer was brought over from Pinsk to design and build the equipment, but he never knew where it would be located. When complete, it was transported to Kfar Giladi and installed secretly by Hashomer.

It is believed that Kfar Giladi has over twenty *slik*s, however the location of each was known only to one or two people. Even today nobody is sure where they are. Hashomer members never divulged the secret even to their closest family. When the wife of one kibbutzik became suspicious about her husband's nightly wanderings, she was sure he was having an affair with a neighbor's wife and insisted on a divorce. Despite this he never revealed the truth.

Torah reached up and took a small package from a shelf. It contained a tiny pearl-handled pistol. The story was that, many years ago, some Arabs arrived at the kibbutz water well intent on causing trouble. Yehudit Hurvitz, the young wife of one of the original founders, was on guard. As they approached, she stood firmly, gun raised, and demanded that they leave. For centuries of Moslem rule no Jew had ever pointed a weapon at an Arab. Much to her – and everyone else's – surprise, they turned and left.

Some days later the kibbutz had an unexpected visitor. It was the mukhtar from the local village together with a few of his tribesmen. He had come, he said, to meet the woman who had confronted his men a few days earlier. On greeting Yehudit he presented her with a package. Inside was the pearl-handled pistol Torah had shown me. He said he was honored to meet Yehudit as she had shown such bravery; he gave her the gun in acknowledgment of her unique courage. On receiving it she vowed never to leave Kfar Giladi, a promise she kept all her life.

No one on the kibbutz knew of the existence of this cache until 1996. Torah's father revealed the secret shortly before he died. Tourists can now visit the *slik*, a powerful reminder of a heroic and dramatic period of history.

The Leopard

Depiction of leopard at the Shrine of the Leopards

Leopards have figured in Hebrew culture for thousands of years. Several references appear in the Bible, such as "Can the Ethiopian change his skin, or the leopard his spots?" (Jeremiah 13:22) alluding to man's inability to change, and "The leopard shall sleep with the kid" (Isaiah 11:6) – an optimistic view of a peaceful future. The leopard is also mentioned in the Song of Songs.

Many places both in Israel and all over the Middle East are named after the animal, such as Nimrah and Beth-Nimrah (from "*namer*" – leopard), located in what was once Moab. In the Golan there is the Mountain of the Leopards, and a valley entering the Dead Sea from the east is called "Valley of the Little Leopard." From this one can infer that in years gone by these animals

had much more of a presence, roaming freely not only in Israel but throughout the Middle East, from Saudi Arabia to Turkey.

Further compelling evidence came from a visit with my guide Alon to Bikaat Uvda. There we saw the Shrine of the Leopards, dating from approximately 6,000 BCE and where people worshipped until about 3,000 BCE, which indicated that the leopard once held a significant role in the spiritual life of the people.

We traveled along the route linking the Dead Sea with Eilat. There, at the side of the road, largely unprotected, was a roughly marked off area of earth containing sixteen depictions of animals – each created from triangular stones embedded in the earth forming their outlines. Fifteen faced east – these were leopards judging by the shape of their heads and their distinctive long, curved tails. The other faced west and was a type of antelope. For me, used to viewing archaeological artefacts in museums, it was very special to walk unsupervised among these unique forms and marvel at their creation with not another soul around.

Today the numbers of this magnificent large cat have hugely diminished to the extent that only about eighteen survive in Israel. In Syria, Jordan and Lebanon they have been completely eradicated.

This decline resulted from climate change, population growth, the destruction of their natural habitat and hunting. The Crusaders put an end to lions in the Middle East, while the widespread introduction of firearms in the late nineteenth century and the growing popularity of hunting as "sport" exacerbated the problem. This was particularly prevalent during the British Mandate when it was "awfully fashionable" to chase and kill wild animals in order to hang trophies on walls.

When Israel was established, the law was altered to protect wild animals but it still permitted some form of hunting. However, in 2010 hunting was banned, except where necessary for the protection of agriculture or livestock. Israel's commitment to nature conservation can in fact be traced back to the book of Genesis, which stressed the essential link between humanity (*adam*) and the earth (*adamah*), underlining man's responsibility for its preservation.

We next traveled to the far north of Israel to seek another leopard story. I was overwhelmed by the beauty of the countryside and its rugged, thickly wooded hills, deep valleys, lush green foliage and a proliferation of wild flowers.

In the mountain range close to the Ridge of Tyre we caught our first glimpse of the Cave of the Leopards, named Arab el Aramshe by the Bedouin. We clambered down from the top of a ridge and suddenly found ourselves on the rim of the cave. The view was spectacular, with a sheer drop of a thousand feet to the valley below.

Leopard cave landscape

Leopards were feared, as they attacked both humans and livestock. The villagers here devised a cunning scheme to trap these predators. The women wove a strong net from goats' hair which was placed on the ground and hidden by undergrowth. A rope secured the net at one end of the cave and the other end was held by a group of men who lay concealed in the bushes.

The villagers tethered a baby goat in the cave and waited for a leopard to come. Eventually one arrived, on hearing the kid bleating for its mother. A lookout signaled to the men below. When the animal was near enough, they pulled the net tight to trap the animal and then all the villagers joined forces to stone it to death.

Considering the small numbers that now exist, it is an anomaly that the leopard still features predominantly in the iconography of Israel. In 1994, silver coins were struck by the government showing the animal surrounded by a text from the Song of Songs. In 2011, the Israel Postal Company printed a set of stamps illustrating leopards for the World Wildlife Fund.

Stories about leopards have also become part of Israeli folklore. One tells of an incident that supposedly happened some two hundred years ago. In the Jerusalem hills stood three villages: Abu Ghosh, Ein Nakuba and Saris. Mostly these villages were in a state of hostility. One night a small girl from Saris was playing outside, but when her mother called her the child did not respond. The mother searched but was unable to find her, sought the assistance of neighbors who in desperation turned to the surrounding villages for help.

All the menfolk gathered and, carrying torches, searched all night – but to no avail. Early the next morning they enlisted the help of trackers, who found the child's footprints alongside those of several wolves. They came to the tragic conclusion that she must have been devoured by the wolves. They also found the footprints of a leopard nearby, which compounded their fears.

They followed these tracks that eventually led to a cave. There they found the child alive, sleeping quietly in a corner. The leopard was lying nearby, guarding her. On seeing the men approach it fled. The child awoke to tell the astonishing tale of how she had been saved by the leopard that had protected her from the marauding wolves.

This cave is called Me'arat el Nimr – The Cave of the Leopard. Whether true or apocryphal, this fable places the leopard in a heroic role rather than the usual one of an aggressive predator.

In 2007 one of Israel's few remaining leopards achieved notoriety when Reuters reported that a forty-five-year-old Israeli, Arthur de Mosh from Sde Boker, was woken from his sleep by the sound of growling and found a leopard in his bedroom trying to catch his pet cat. Our hero bravely rescued the pet from the animal's clutches and wrestled the leopard to the ground, where it lay in a catatonic state until help arrived. Arthur's cat recovered from its traumatic experience; the leopard was found to be suffering from malnutrition. It was taken away for medical tests, including (naturally) a CAT scan, before being released into a nature reserve.

After writing this story I jokingly said to Alon, "Now you have to find me a real leopard!" "No problem," he replied, so the next day we drove down south to the Hai Bar Nature Reserve. Alon had been responsible for setting up this center in 1966 with the objective of restoring extant animals mentioned in the Bible to the land of Israel.

He introduced me to a magnificent leopard which came within twelve inches of my camera. Fortunately, I was well protected by a heavy glass partition. But the thrill of seeing it at such close quarters prowling back and forth, observing its rippling muscles and almost feeling its breath, made me realize why these creatures were held in such awe and why they had once had such a prominent place in the lives of our ancestors.

Meeting my leopard

The Lido

Hand-painted mural in the "spa"

At the northern tip of the Dead Sea, close to Jericho, lies a derelict graffiti-covered concrete building surrounded by wasteland.

This was the site of the Lido, an elegant tourist spot built in the 1930s to which the wealthier residents of Jericho and Jerusalem would come and have lunch, smoke a water pipe (*nargila*), take a dip in the Dead Sea and enjoy the natural splendors of the area.

Appearances can be deceptive, however. On entering the building you come upon a vast circular room, open to the skies, where your eyes are greeted by an immense mural over three hundred feet long, stretching along the entire perimeter of the room. It depicts the topography of Israel in muted colors of ochre, terra-cotta and browns – the colors of the landscape itself.

Geographical features from the coast of Lebanon down to the Negev are featured, with names carefully executed in English calligraphy and interspersed with illustrations of buildings and small villages.

This artwork was completed forty years ago, by a reserve soldier in the Israeli army named Kohavi, the design being based on a Crusader map and printed in 1475 by Lucas Brandis.

The mural is punctured by several large holes – the result of Jordanian bombardment. These add a surreal dimension to the artwork, illustrating a dramatic point in history while creating natural frames through which to view the real world outside.

On one side of the room steps lead down to what was once a jetty, just feet away from the building. From here visitors could alight onto small boats that would take them for a leisurely tour of the Dead Sea. In those days its salty waters lapped gently against the steps, but today the water is about half a mile away and barely visible.

The Dead Sea's surface has been reduced by a third since the 1960s. Over the same period the water level has gone from 1293 feet to 1400 feet below sea level, caused by the reduction of water flowing into the sea from the Jordan River, as well as evaporation of the water from extreme heat.

It is sad to see the abandoned remains of what was once an elegant spa. But these faded images of a colonial past make it easy to conjure up the spirit of those early days when Arab sheiks and panama-hatted gentlemen and their ladies in elegant gowns came to see and be seen.

It would be nice if some entrepreneur could restore the building as a tourist attraction and raise

Your eyes are greeted by an immense mural over three hundred feet long.

awareness of the problems facing the Dead Sea. Nature has certainly taken its toll over the years, but in this land of occasional miracles I would like to think that nothing is impossible.

Lido with hole in the wall caused by bombardment

Life's a Beach

Thirty years ago I visited Tel Aviv regularly to promote business between Britain and Israel. I stayed in a beachside hotel and, when I could get up early enough, would take a walk along the seashore.

What I remember most about those times were the groups of elderly people, skins tanned like chestnuts, congregating in the sea, chatting and solving the world's problems. They had mastered the art of swimming vertically, which I always found impressive. After their deliberations they moved to the sand and embarked on twenty minutes of keep-fit exercises. One day I joined in and am embarrassed to say that I only survived for five minutes as it was seriously intense!

When Tel Aviv first officially became a city in 1934 this passion for beach life was not shared by all. Meir Dizengoff, the first mayor of Tel Aviv, was recorded as saying "Jews don't like to bathe in the sea." He and the founding fathers planned to develop heavy industry along the coastline, but fortunately Tel Avivians thought otherwise. They flocked daily to the sea and his plans were abandoned.

During the 1950s the beach became less popular, due to sewage pollution in the sea and extensive building of high-rise hotels along the front. Today, however, it has regained popularity and is once more the place for everyone to come and indulge in their favorite activities.

Meir Dizengoff said,
"Jews don't like to
bathe in the sea."

Israel technically has four seasons, but in reality summer slips imperceptibly into winter. This year I was still wearing sandals and a T-shirt on December 1, with the temperature at 27 degrees. Autumn simply does not happen so beachside activities can continue year round. In March it may be windy and cold, but within hours the sun shines, winter turns into summer and everyone heads back to the beach. This is the place where early-morning hordes of predominantly over-fif-

ties take their daily constitutional, striding forward with the determination to arrive first.

Israel's Mediterranean coastline stretches 123 miles from Rosh Hanikra in the north, to Ashkelon in the south. Everywhere one sees people engaging in the ubiquitous *matkot* (beach tennis) and water sports, but it is the promenade that teems with yoga and tai chi enthusiasts, cyclists and gymnasts all trying to perfect their skills. Working out by the beach, smelling the salty air and listening to the waves, is far removed from the experience of running on a treadmill in a gym. The activity transforms into one with a spiritual dimension.

There are specialist beaches for different groups. The religiously observant are provided

Where's my lens?

with gender-specific beaches. On one side you see fully dressed women sitting on chairs with their feet in the water, surrounded by a great number of small children, while at a respectable distance, religious men try their hand, or perhaps more realistically, their feet, at swimming.

Some beaches are reserved for gays and lesbians and there are even those where your dog can run with impunity. The web lists those designated places where dogs can frolic without a leash, for apparently "sandy paws make for happy dogs."

Comes evening however, the beaches assume a different atmosphere. Particularly on Fridays when, as dusk falls, hundreds of young people gather in circles, playing drums, flutes and guitars. They dance, sing and drink for hours until the sun goes down. This festive ritual, which began twenty years ago, is something of an "alterna-tive" welcoming of the Sabbath – evocative of the peace-loving gatherings of hippies in the 1960s.

I have always loved the seaside. As a small child we were evacuated from Manchester to Blackpool to escape the German bombs. My earliest memories are of playing on the sand with a bucket and spade and riding on donkeys. In later years we regularly took weekend day trips to nearby St. Annes, where we played on the sand hills and ate egg, cress and sand sandwiches. I always thought that was why they were called "sandwiches."

Today I divide my time between London and Jerusalem. I love Jerusalem, but would enjoy it even more were it located on the beach. This will never happen of course, so I guess I shall just have to be satisfied with continuing to take day trips, much as I did as a child.

Fishermen, Tel Aviv

Mahane Yehuda Market

General view of Mahane Yehuda

Markets have held a fascination for me since early childhood when I would accompany my father to work, he being a market trader. I loved the sounds, the smells, the sights and the camaraderie, and a visit to Mahane Yehuda, the Jewish market in Jerusalem, brings memories flooding back. The language may be different, as is some of the produce, but much remains the same.

One can still hear the traditional banter and cries of vendors competing to sell their wares, and breathe in the aroma of exotic spices. In the last few years enterprising café owners have taken advantage of the plentiful supply of fresh produce and opened new eating places. There is even a fish 'n' chips café – hard to imagine this translating well into Israeli society, but apparently it does!

The market is a photographer's dream – so much color, life and vitality with fascinating characters to complete the picture. Stalls piled high with just about everything imaginable include specialist traders selling halva, olive oil, spices and cheeses. In recent years the market has had a face lift with new boutiques replacing some of

The market is a
photographer's
dream – color,
life and vitality.

Selling strawberries

to this the boys whose job it is to clear away the debris. They too seem to find a passageway to transport their huge loads of cardboard cartons.

No visit is complete without stopping for breakfast at Eli Mizrahi's. Here is where the literati and other regulars come to sit, smoke, chat and watch the world go by. His ever-present smile and welcoming hug makes you feel like you have come home.

Trader, Mahane Yehuda

the older tradesmen, but it still retains an energy and a charm all of its own.

The market was once considered a power base for the support of right-wing parties. No politician worth his salt would miss the opportunity to visit on the eve of elections to solicit votes for his party. Posters of Menachem Begin adorn the walls even today.

Trying to walk through the market especially on a Friday morning can be something of a challenge. The elderly push unceremoniously through the crowds with their ubiquitous trolleys, gesticulating and talking with their elbows. Stallholders somehow manage to maneuver their way while loaded down with crates of fresh supplies. Add

Matkot

Practicing at Gordon Beach

A visit to any Israeli beach is unique. No longer the rhythm of waves gently lapping against the seashore, rather a "*pok pok*" sound of ball being repeatedly hit against hard wooden bat sounding like a frenzied army of woodpeckers.

It is *matkot* – Israel's leading national sport alongside eating falafel, gesturing with the hands and shouting rather a lot.

Large swathes of sand once happily occupied by families with small children have been appropriated by devotees of this fast-paced game, ranging from elderly men in underwear not meant to be seen in public, to macho youngsters trying to outdo their peers.

To stroll along the beach today requires not only nerves of steel but also the agility to be able to wend and weave to avoid being hit by the fast-moving lethal rubber balls. The curious thing, however, is that there are no rules to this game. It is totally non-competitive. No one scores against the other. The aim is in fact the opposite, one of complete cooperation with your partner to enable him to return the ball back to you.

Israel has yet to achieve supremacy in the field

of international sport. I believe that when *matkot* is included in a future Olympics, they may be in with a strong chance.

This is not such a pipe dream – think back to the 1940s, the years of Esther Williams and Synchronized Swimming while Simultaneously Smiling – would we ever then have considered it a viable addition to the world of gymnastics as it is now? Watch this space…

Israel's national sport alongside eating falafel, gesturing with the hands and shouting rather a lot.

Balletic on the beach

Amnon
waiting
for
visitors

The *Matkot* Museum

Amnon sitting in the street

My inquiries into *matkot*, the ball game played regularly on Tel Aviv's beaches, led me to the discovery that a small museum unbeknown to most people had been dedicated to this sport in Tel Aviv. I went to see it for myself. In a narrow street in Neve Zedek I found "Amnon the Cannon," tanned and fit, sitting on a chair in the street underneath a sign promoting his "shrine."

The only child of Yemenite parents, Amnon, born 1944, began playing *matkot* at age six. He served in the army until retirement at forty-five, and on receiving a pension he resolved to follow his dream. He never married but instead devoted his entire life to the game that has given him an alternative "family" of like-minded enthusiasts.

Not a day goes by without his going to the beach to play.

Some years ago he met another devotee, Morris the Great, so called because of his sporting expertise. Between them they developed the plan for the museum.

Across an open courtyard and up an iron staircase you are led to this unexpected and fascinating world of *matkot*. This is Amnon's apartment. A bed stands in a corner, but this and every inch of wall space is covered with a display of three hundred bats – wooden ones for playing, and decorative ones in ceramic or marble. A *matkot*-shaped table is piled high with awards, certificates and photographs, plus albums of carefully recorded

Amnon in his empire

newspaper articles. Balls of all sizes and colors are dotted around. A *matkot* clock ticks slowly away on the wall.

Amnon's passion and enthusiasm is infectious. He is affectionately regarded as the father of *matkot* to all the players. "I am living my dream," he said. "Every day I do exactly what I love most – how lucky can I be?"

He then took me aside and quietly confided that his second great passion was music, in particular the vocals of Dean Martin and Connie Francis, popular crooners of the 1950s. "Have you heard of them?" he asked. "Do you like music?"

When I told him that I knew of them and that I was studying singing, his face lit up and he urged me to perform for him. Was this my big chance? A debut solo before a captive audience found me rendering a version of the "Habanera" from Carmen, molto fortissimo. There stood Amnon the Cannon, his face only inches away from mine, holding my gaze with his piercing and unblinking blue-grey eyes.

I would dearly like to think that his expression was one of pure, unadulterated joy, but more realistically suspect that he was like a rabbit caught in headlights by this onslaught of Bizet at such close quarters.

Such are the unforgettable cameos that make life richer.

Facing the onslaught of Bizet

Today she employs and trains seven Bedouin women.

Medicine Woman

Mariam

People throughout the world readily adapt to the most inhospitable of climates. The Inuit survive the frozen wastes of the Arctic, the Aborigines the sweltering heat of Australia.

In the Middle East, the Bedouin acclimatized to their harsh environment. As a nomadic community they had to be totally self-sufficient as regards both food and medicine. Over generations they learned where to find water and which plants could provide nourishment or be used for healing. Their knowledge was often gained by watching the behavior of animals that knew instinctively where to seek water, which plants were edible and which could be used medicinally.

Near Beersheba I met Mariam Abu Rakeek.

Born and raised in her family tent, she remembers as a child watching her grandmother chop up different herbs to mix with natural oils. She produced potions and salves that, in conjunction with her skill as a spiritual healer, cured a variety of ailments.

Mariam was a remarkable girl. Coming from a society that traditionally placed little value on educating females, she determined to go to Britain to study for a degree in marketing. Her understanding family financed the trip. She gained her degree and had the opportunity to observe how cosmetics were promoted in the West, quickly identifying a growing trend toward chemical-free organic products.

On returning to Israel she was urged to marry, but Mariam was reluctant to follow the traditional path of an arranged union. She lived with her parents but gradually developed ideas for starting a business. Initially, she acted as a representative for an overseas cosmetics firm, but soon realized that she possessed the skills to make her own products based on her family's traditional recipes.

Her grandmother had reservations about Mariam "selling" her knowledge, for, as a healer, she considered such "gifts" as God given, not to be exploited commercially. Eventually, however, she recognized Mariam's ability to help others cure their medical problems and encouraged her to proceed.

Her father, recognizing her dedication, provided land where she could base her activities. During the first year she worked alone making soap. Then she branched out into oils. Nothing was packaged – customers brought their own containers for Mariam to fill, and so the business

Collection of wild organic herbs

developed. Today she employs and trains seven Bedouin women.

Together they collect wild plants and seeds. *Nigella sativa* – mentioned in the book of Isaiah and known in English as fennel flower or black cumin – is used as a flavoring and preservative with claims that it can treat asthma and high blood pressure and can improve liver function. Black cumin oil is widely acknowledged as a "cure-all" in most traditional Arab healing. Bitter apple has been used for centuries as an anti-inflammatory and analgesic, and *Artemisia*, for its antiseptic and anti-spasmodic properties.

Camel milk is an essential ingredient in Mariam's product range as the basis for one of her organic soaps. It can also alleviate conditions such as allergies and diabetes.

Mariam told me that she is on a mission to provide work opportunities and to give her employees self-respect and a feeling of independence. She constantly experiments with new products and has ventured where many from her background might fear to tread.

Mariam is unique, combining a love for her religion (she had just returned from Mecca when we met) with a positive outlook as to what the future can hold for Bedouin women. I heard her speak to two busloads of Israeli women. They were captivated, as was I, by her enthusiasm and commitment. They eagerly bought everything and emptied the shelves of products.

Mariam is a rare phenomenon in one of the most traditional societies in the world, but her example is an indication that new directions can be taken. Meeting her was a privilege.

Men's Headwear

Hats on parade in Jerusalem shop

The Talmud states that Jewish men should cover their heads "in order that the fear of heaven may be upon them." Men must not walk more than "four cubits" with their heads uncovered. I seriously doubt that many men these days know the measurement of a cubit which, for your edification, is 45.72 centimeters (approximately).

But this esoteric piece of information is irrelevant today as most authorities deem that men should cover their heads at *all* times, presumably obviating the necessity to have a tape measure at the ready to measure a cubit.

Nowhere is it written that men have to wear hats. A *kippah*, or skullcap, is sufficient. But over the years it has become customary to wear a hat outside the home, with some rabbis insisting that a *kippah* must be worn underneath it, just to be sure.

Among the Hasidim, with over thirty main sects and many subsects, subtle differences in headgear, known only to the cognoscenti, identify to which group a man belongs. Take the familiar

black fedora, worn by religious Ashkenazi Jews since the 1940s and 50s. Sometimes the width of the brim is the determining factor, or the specific way the hat is "pinched" – the most favored being the "Lubavitch pinch," with three dents in the crown, made popular by the late Lubavitcher Rebbe and called the "yeshivish" style. Others make only one pinch in the top – or leave it rounded.

For some reason younger men wear these hats in a size much too small for them, perched precariously on the top of the head. There is no official explanation for this; presumably it is a fashion statement.

Apart from the fedora, men can choose to wear a Samet, Kolpik, Kutchma or Kashket – each sounding like exotic casserole dishes but in reality these are hats originating from different Eastern European countries.

The one universally recognized is the *shtreimel*. There is speculation about its origins. One suggestion is that a decree was established in Poland,

Men can
choose
to wear
a Samet,
Kolpik,
Kutchma
or Kashket

Protecting their hats

requiring Jews to be identified, and insulted, by wearing a "tail" on their heads. The rabbis ingeniously devised a hat, comprising animal tails from beaver, sable or stone marten and wrapped clockwise to resemble a crown. Ironically what started out as an affront was transformed into an object to be worn with pride. Today a *shtreimel* is the special gift a Hasid will give to his son on his wedding day.

These can cost up to $6,000. In 2008 two warring subsects of the Viznitz group – the Mendelists and the Yisraelists – engaged in street fights in Bnei Brak over the question of who should be their leader. Their objective was to capture as many *shtreimel*s as possible from their opponents and bargain for their return. The police were involved and people were injured and hospitalized during the fracas.

Today, however, another serious threat confronts the *shtreimel* wearer in Israel. A law has been brought in to ban the import of animal pelts from the Far East, as it was found that the rearing practices involved considerable cruelty to animals. "Fur flies over threat to Hasidic headwear," ran the headlines.

However, some leading rabbis came out in support of the ban, saying that for one to wear an animal pelt is very much against the spirit and the law of Judaism, where it clearly states that it is wrong to cause animals needless pain.

Opponents of the measure are up in arms – this time not literally. The law carries a one-year prison sentence for those who break it. There is no doubt that in Jerusalem men's hats are highly valued. Evidence of this is apparent on any rainy day in the city. The streets are filled with men in black coats wearing plastic bags over their expensive headwear. It is a sight to behold. Curiously, I have never once seen a man holding an umbrella in a downpour – they only seem concerned about their hats.

For some unaccountable reason, when I resort to wearing a plastic bag on my head in London when it rains I get some particularly odd looks from passersby and expressions of horror from my family, who scurry to the other side of the street rather than acknowledge that I am connected to then in any way. Strange how some customs just don't travel well.

The Music Man

On May 8, 2015, I, Ruth Corman, previously believed to be of sound mind and body, found myself standing on a rostrum before a fifty-piece orchestra, in Israel, conducting a left-handed version of the opening movement of Dvorak's New World Symphony. No, this was not a dream. It was absolutely true; it really happened.

Earlier, a friend had phoned to say she had a story that might be of interest and suggested I visit the Ma'ale Adumim Music Conservatory to learn of their work in the field of musical education. The principal, Benjamin Shapira, and I exchanged emails to confirm my visit. Eventually the date arrived. Unfortunately I had had a particularly exhausting day and when it was time to

go it was the last thing I wanted to do, but having promised, I could not bring myself to cancel. Had I done so, I would have missed out on a unique encounter, as the visit proved to be one of those memorable occasions when you meet a person you instantly recognize as extra special – someone with the ability to transform lives.

Benjamin was born into a musical family, At age three, he was playing the piano, and by five he began studying the cello. He was drawn to this instrument but could not, at that age, articulate the reason why. Today, he acknowledges that he loves the cello because, he says, it is the instrument that most resembles the human voice.

Around the age of eleven his burgeoning talent

was confirmed by the world renowned violinist, Isaac Stern, who selected him to join a group of talented youngsters and train at the Jerusalem Music Center. Here he remained until eighteen, when he entered the army as one of only five recruits admitted to the IDF Outstanding Musicians' Program. He was a regular soldier for six hours a day but practiced the cello and studied music for the remainder of his time.

After army service and university, Benjamin was offered a place to study for a master's degree at Yale University. His stellar career began, following a debut at Carnegie Hall where he played Bach's complete *Set of Suites for Solo Cello*. The press reviews were outstanding and from then on he was in constant demand worldwide.

He completed his doctorate at Rutgers University and eventually was recognized by the US government as an "Artist of National Interest." He subsequently accepted the position of orchestral director with the University of Wisconsin, Platteville.

It was then that Benjamin had something of an epiphany with the realization that his future lay not in the United States but in Israel. He decided to return in order to give back something to his country and developed a plan to provide top-class musical education for youngsters who would normally never have access to such tuition. A magnificent state of the art music school was built by the authorities in Ma'ale Adumim and in 2007 children from all walks of life – secular

A group of string players

and religious, and from all cultural and ethnic backgrounds – arrived on the doorstep.

Benjamin advocates the method used in the United States where, from day one, each child becomes part of a social group – the orchestra – regardless of his or her ability. There are several levels of orchestra, from beginners to advanced, by which time they play together for eight hours a week, with two hours practice every day as well as a private theory lesson.

Remarkably, in only seven years, the school has achieved significant success. Their harp players have performed with the Israel Philharmonic Orchestra, a string quartet has played at the president's house and history repeated itself when a young percussionist was accepted for the IDF Outstanding Musicians' Program. The school's top orchestra has won prizes in Slovakia and in 2015 they were invited to perform at Carnegie Hall.

A great deal has been written about the power of music to aid cognitive development in youngsters. Several of Benjamin's students were undisciplined, disruptive and isolated when they arrived. However, the system he uses encourages cooperation and develops a sense of responsibility and commitment to a shared purpose. The self-esteem that inevitably follows enhances all areas of the child's life. It instils positive attitudes, builds confidence and improves social adjustment.

When I visited the conservatory to meet the children, they were initially a little shy but soon opened up and were able to express their feelings. It was very moving. Some had begun playing in regular schools as part of the conservatory's outreach program. They told me of their problems in being regarded as "different" by the other kids and how they found it difficult to make friends and frequently felt lonely. They said that they had often resorted to pretending to misbehave in order to be accepted as part of their peer group.

However, on arrival at the conservatory they were immediately part of a warm, open family with whom they had much in common. One girl said, "I cannot live without music." After our meeting she sent me an email in which she said that, after talking to me, she reflected on why she enjoyed music so much. She wrote: "Listening to the concert today my whole body reacted when I heard the music. I had shivers of excitement, so I guess that my brain and my heart just love what music does to me. It is exactly the same when I play the violin."

One student called music her "best friend." Another said that it had changed his personality. From being lonely and rejected, music presented him with a new world of challenges and possibilities. I must say that these young musicians were extraordinarily impressive.

I myself understand something of the power of music, having taken up singing at a comparatively late age. I love the discipline of learning the techniques of voice production. More than that, it is quite simply that, however tired I might feel when I start singing, I rapidly become energized and feel supremely happy. In my view music should be prescribed by every health service. It is just like taking a "happy pill."

Now back to my debut as an orchestral conductor. As I descended the rostrum one teacher remarked how competent I was and asked for how long I had been conducting. I was able to tell him in all honesty that my entire career had spanned five and a half minutes. But, unexpectedly, another career possibility has opened up for me. Benjamin begins to transform my life too.

He has invited me to perform with him and a group of young cellists, when I will sing the aria from Bachianas Brasileiras No 5 by Villa Lobos.

I have never been one to refuse a challenge. However in this case, it might be more appropriate to suggest that my eagerness to climb this particular mountain might be a perfect example of "Fools rush in where angels fear to tread." We shall have to wait and see…

There were youngsters who, through no fault of their own, missed the opportunity to serve in the army.

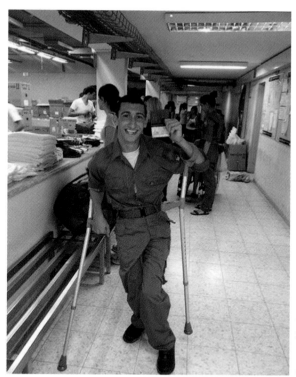

A Need for Special People

Great in uniform

It was David Ben-Gurion, Israel's first minister, who said that the Israel Defense Forces (IDF) were not only the means of defending the country but were also highly significant in developing Israeli society.

Since the beginning of the state, huge numbers of immigrants arrived on Israel's shores from all over the globe. They had to learn a new language, find housing and employment and adjust to a completely new way of life.

Various means have been employed to help them integrate but by far the best method of absorbing the newcomers proved to be for them to join the army. This has acted as an effective "social leveler," reinforcing the egalitarian principles upon which the country was founded. Today, recruits from all backgrounds go through lengthy training procedures which help them develop so-

cial identities that transcend the previously held attitudes of different social and economic groups.

Army service is the time when lifelong friendships are forged and skills acquired that lead to wider employment opportunities. In addition, an informal network results in preferential treatment for former soldiers in the job market. Nowadays, there are a few Israelis who choose to leave the country to avoid their national service. However some 80 percent of Israel's young people recognize military service as a duty that they are willing and indeed proud to undertake.

At the age of seventeen, potential recruits undergo a series of tests to assess their profile. This determines their suitability for the various roles in the army. The highest profilers become fighter pilots and parachutists. At the other end of the scale are the "jobniks," who perform more basic tasks.

Sadly, however, there were youngsters who, through no fault of their own, missed the opportunity to serve in the army, such as those classified as having "special needs." Teenagers with hearing or sight impairment, or with physical or mental difficulties, grew up aware that they were not the same as everyone else. At the age of eighteen they saw their friends and contemporaries join the army, while they themselves were turned down. This left them with a strong feeling of rejection and a lack of self-esteem.

Fortunately this changed in 2004. Colonel Ariel Almog had the vision to found a project that would integrate these youngsters into the IDF on a special four-year voluntary program, during which time they play a valuable role in the service of their country. At the end of this period, it was noticeable how much more easily they were absorbed into the general workforce. Colonel Almog's project, called "Great in Uniform," clearly demonstrated how much the IDF could benefit from the contribution of these special youngsters.

Jobs are allocated according to an individual's ability. For example, those with autism prove to have a unique talent for focusing on electronic maps and being able to identify even the smallest changes, an activity that most non-autistic recruits would find difficult. The IDF Intelligence Unit has had significant successes thanks to the singular contribution of their autistic soldiers.

Regular soldiers take pride in the achievements of their "special needs" group, who become a welcome addition at a number of military bases. In turn, the advantage to the recruits is inestimable. Their confidence grows as they realize that they are genuinely making a difference. As Major Motti Dayan explained, "They are an inseparable part of our unit and are just like any other soldiers."

For some, joining the army may be the first time that they leave home alone, but they quickly learn to become independent and adapt to their new roles. Like all the other soldiers, they are taught the values of the IDF through educational programs and tour the country, learning its history.

Toward the end of their training they embark on a special trek that culminates in the ceremony when they receive their berets. It was deeply moving for me to see their evident pride when they put on their berets for the first time and then saluted their commanding officer. For them and their watching families this represented the culmination of a dream many thought could never be realized. Said one recruit: "I've been waiting so long for this. It will remain with me for the rest of my life."

To see the joy of these soldiers and that of their families made me realize the value of this unique project. It enables this "special" group of people to realize their potential, giving them dignity and the chance to hold their heads high and feel equal among their peers. This is an aspect of the IDF that, sadly, is largely unknown outside the country.

"I've been waiting so long for this. It will remain with me for the rest of my life."

> The tranquility is interrupted only by birdsong, the rustling of foliage in the breeze and the ever-present sound of water as it tumbles over rocks.

Youngsters at a pool, Ein Feshkha

Oasis of Tranquility

Occasionally in life you come upon a place that, for a variety of reasons, exerts a magical pull on your emotions. One such spot is Ein Feshkha, totally unique if only for the fact that is the lowest nature reserve in the world, situated almost fourteen hundred feet below sea level, on the northern edge of the Dead Sea.

Imagine a paradise of semitropical plants – tamarisk, oleander and papyrus – flourishing in a natural oasis, crisscrossed with streams of fresh running water. Numerous pools are alive with frogs, toads and five species of fish – one of which, a type of St. Peter's fish, is found nowhere else on earth. Sights and sounds harmoniously merge to create a lasting impression – the tranquility interrupted only by birdsong, the rustling of foliage in the breeze and the ever-present sound of water as it tumbles over rocks.

All of this set against the majestic backdrop of the Judean hills on one side and the Dead Sea on the other. It is the gradual shrinkage of the Dead Sea, estimated at three feet per year, that has resulted in the growth of Ein Feshkha, to the extent that it now covers 124 acres. The decline in the level of the Dead Sea exposed soft clay rocks that had sunk into the seabed. Flowing springs from deep underground sources cut through these layers, creating mini canyons and a unique microhabitat.

It is astonishing to come across this paradise in an arid desert with virtually no rainfall and

Stream at Ein Feshkha

seek ways of using the water for local agricultural purposes while, at the same time, maintaining the pristine nature of the reserve, restoring the waterways and replenishing its fish stocks.

Over hot, sweet herbal tea and seven-year-old hard cheese (a local specialty), I sat and talked with Eed, a Bedouin who has worked there since 1967. He told me how Jews, Bedouin and Palestinians work side by side to ensure the safe future of the oasis. Eed and his friends are truly blessed. They are living their dream and seeing the realization of their efforts to preserve this little slice of heaven.

so close to the Dead Sea which, because of its high salinity, supports no life other than a few microbes.

The site attracts a variety of animal life – the striped hyena, wolf, jackal, porcupine, caracal and mongoose. Birds making their homes here include the nightingale, kingfisher, great reed warbler and the unusually named Arabian babbler. Insects include the Middle Eastern jewel beetle, which lives its entire life in the tamarisk tree.

A special area is set aside with pools and walks for families with young children – a great opportunity to introduce them to nature.

Archaeologists state that this site supported a farm from the first century BCE that included an industrial site probably for the production of balsam perfume. The Jewish historian Flavius Josephus described the area as "the most fertile spot in Judea." In Roman and Byzantine times wild sugarcane, henna and sycamore fig flourished.

In 72–73 CE, the springs at Ein Feshkha provided fresh drinking water for the Roman legions besieging Masada, but since then little use has been made of the water apart from small irrigation projects.

Today experts from the Israel Water Authority

Pathway at Ein Feshkha

Oranges: A Bittersweet Story

Oranges in the sun

The orange is the icon probably most widely associated with Israel. Years ago as director of the British-Israel Chamber of Commerce my job was to approach British businessman and encourage them to trade with Israel. When asked what they knew about the country they would inevitably reply, "They sell oranges and have a crack army." A visitor to Israel in those early years asked a tour guide friend of mine what they did with all those oranges. He replied, "We eat what we can and we can what we can't."

Oranges are not indigenous to the Middle East. The sweet variety came from China, brought to

Portugal by the explorer Vasco De Gama and then on to the Holy Land.

The original citrus plantations were owned by wealthy Arab landowners and by 1845 exports numbered two hundred thousand. In 1850 the philanthropist Sir Moses Montefiore bought plots of land and planted orange groves and thirty-five years later Baron Edmond de Rothschild planted more orchards in developing agricultural settlements such as Petah Tikva. From these early beginnings the production of oranges developed until they became one of Israel's main exports, only superseded in recent years by high technology.

During the British Mandate period oranges

"We eat what we can and we can what we can't."

Prison cell, central Jerusalem

featured in a courageous and tragic event. Two young Jewish fighters, Meir Feinstein (19) and Moshe Barazani (20) were due to be hanged by the British forces on April 21, 1947. Explosives were smuggled into the Central Jerusalem Prison where the boys were being held. Hand grenades were made by the other prisoners and were concealed in hollowed-out oranges.

Their intention was to blow themselves up dramatically next to the hangman's noose. At the last minute, however, their plans had to be changed as the prison rabbi stated that he insisted on standing next to the boys while they awaited execution, so that the last face they would see on earth would be a friendly one. In this event, while in their cell, the boys gave a Bible to their British guard, Thomas Goodwin, who had been kind to them, and asked him to leave and go outside to pray for them.

He went outside. A few minutes later the prison was rocked with a huge explosion and the boys died, blowing themselves up in their cell. Inside the Bible given to Goodwin was a note. Part of it read: "Remember that we stood with dignity and marched with honor. It is better to die with a weapon in your hands than with hands raised in surrender." In 2008 Goodwin's grandson came to Jerusalem, met with Feinstein's family and returned the Bible.

The prison in question was originally a hostel for Russian women pilgrims coming to the Holy Land. It is located in the Russian Compound in Jerusalem, an area containing several buildings of considerable beauty and architectural interest. Once again oranges featured.

In 1964 the Russian government sold most of the compound to the Israeli government and was paid in oranges. It was called the "orange deal." I had heard that it was a box of oranges, but in fact it was a rather large box – to the value of $3.5 million.

In 2012 an agreement was reached to return part of the compound to the Russians. I wonder if the Russians feel obliged to return any of the oranges?

Pesach (Passover)

Visitors to the bakery rolling the dough into rounds

Pesach commemorates the exodus of the Israelites from Egypt. God helped the Children of Israel to escape slavery and flee from Egypt by inflicting ten plagues upon the Egyptians so that eventually Pharaoh agreed to let them go.

The Jews left Egypt in a great hurry and had no time to let their bread rise, so during Pesach no leavened bread is eaten, only a flat bread that does not rise – matzo. It is called the "bread of affliction." Some people enjoy matzo, but for others, including me, it is truly a bread of affliction particularly in the way it affects modern digestive systems.

Religious families clean their homes thor-oughly before Pesach to eliminate every crumb of bread, seeking it out with a candle and a feather. It is also customary to change the dishes and use special ones during this holiday. I recall as a child the sense of occasion on seeing our once-a-year dishes being unwrapped.

Families gather for a "Seder" meal when every father reads the Haggadah, the story of the Exo-dus, to his children so that each one feels that they personally have been released from bondage. The table is set with a platter of symbolic foods and four glasses of wine must be drunk during the meal. The evening ends with the prayer "Next year may we all be in Jerusalem."

Finished shemurah *matzo*

I felt a childlike sense of awe seeing matzo produced traditionally – a link that binds us to our heritage.

This year I was invited to a matzo-baking ceremony at the Karlin Hasidim bakery in Jerusalem. Water was added to *shemurah* (supervised) flour and the dough was kneaded using a metal roller fixed to the wall and operated by two men. When ready, small amounts were handed to each visitor who rolled them into a flat, circular shape with a rolling pin.

These were placed on a long pole and put into a wood-fired oven for three to ten seconds, after which they were carefully lifted out. I was invited to perform this function, not easy in a small, hot and crowded room. The whole process from adding water to producing the matzo must not take more than eighteen minutes; otherwise it begins to rise.

I had never before given thought as to how matzo is made. I was reminded of when, some years ago, a friend's child came to my home for lunch and was astonished to learn that chips (french fries) were made from potatoes and did not just arrive frozen in a plastic bag. I felt that same childlike sense of awe seeing matzo produced traditionally, and recognizing one of those links that binds us to our heritage.

There are few occasions when I would walk fifty minutes in freezing rain and icy winds, but the warm welcome of the Karlin community made it worth the effort. I left carefully carrying my precious three sheets of matzo that I had actually brought into this world. The only downside was when I slipped and fell on the icy pavement and arrived home with three hundred small pieces instead of the requisite three for the Seder meal. Never mind – as they say, it's the experience that counts!

Young Karlin hasidim who showed me how to bake the matzoth

Every
January
thousands
come to
immerse
themselves
in the River
Jordan

Pilgrimage to Israel

Carrying the cross up Via Dolorosa, Jerusalem

The Holy Land, as its name suggests, is exactly that for millions, particularly any follower of the Judeo-Christian tradition – for whom a visit to Israel represents the fulfilment of a dream.

In Biblical times Israelites were commanded to make a pilgrimage to the Temple in Jerusalem for the major festivals of Passover, Shavuot (Pentecost) and Succoth (Tabernacles), but after its destruction this obligation no longer applied.

Jews still visit the Western Wall (the only surviving part of the Temple) and today also visit the tombs of the righteous in Mt. Meron, Safed, Netivot and Hebron. They believe that by praying at these holy places their supplications will be more readily answered.

Christian pilgrims began visiting the Holy Land in the fourth century, encouraged by Helena, the mother of Constantine the Great. In 2013 a record 3.54 million tourists visited Israel. Of these around 1.5 million were Christians. Their first stop is usually Jerusalem where devout followers trace the footsteps of Jesus along the Via Dolorosa in the Old City, some symbolically carrying a heavy wooden cross, stopping to pray at each of the fourteen Stations of the Cross.

They end their walk at the Church of the Holy Sepulchre, where many prostrate themselves on the holy tomb. They also rub cloths over the tomb. I thought at first they were cleaning it, but it seems that they do this so that their piece of fabric will absorb its holiness.

Christmas is the time to visit Bethlehem, where Manger Square is packed to capacity. At other times pilgrims travel to the Sea of Galilee or make the journey to be baptized in the waters of the River Jordan at Qasr-Al-Yahud.

This is the spot at which the ancient Israelites, after forty years in the wilderness, crossed into the Holy Land and where, according to the Gospels, Jesus was baptized. Every January thousands arrive to immerse themselves in the sacred waters of the Jordan at the end of the Christian Epiphany. I went to see this ceremony for myself.

"Get there early to ensure a good seat," we were told, so we duly left Jerusalem at 7:30 A.M. to arrive forty minutes later at a parking lot on a windswept stretch of nothing very much outside Jericho. It was very cold. After twenty minutes of waiting, a bus took us to the baptism site.

All seats near the stairs leading to the water were already occupied, so visitors sat in front of an outdoor screen waiting optimistically for something to appear. As it was so chilly I walked vigorously around looking for people to photograph and talk to. This was the day when Eastern Orthodox and Israeli Arab Christians paid their respects. The Ethiopians and Copts were coming the next day. I met Masud, a Catholic from Jaffa, who came annually with six busloads of family and friends. Groups of nuns sat in circles chatting or embroidering icons. Priests dressed in long robes walked around looking important. I met Greeks, Romanians, Bulgarians and Russians.

The event has a festive atmosphere – akin to a holiday outing. Eventually at 11:30 A.M. things began to happen. A parade of assorted dignitaries arrived with musical accompaniment from pipe bands and youth groups. A priest gave a benediction and white doves were released.

That year, 2013, the waters of the Jordan flowed dangerously high following heavy rain so no-

body was allowed to enter the river. But pilgrims seemed content to buy bottles of "Genuine Scented Jordan River Water." I never discovered why it had to be scented, or indeed what they would do with it once they arrived home. Others departed happily carrying certificates, signed by a priest, to attest to their baptisms on that day. The fact that they had not actually "immersed" did not seem to matter. They may have even experienced a slight sense of relief – the water was not only dangerous but also freezing.

Such devotional activities seemed of great significance, allowing believers to express their commitment to their faith, and demonstrating the centrality of water both as a purifying source and symbolizing the most essential element of life.

Nun sewing an icon

Pomegranates

Pomegranate

One of the earliest known archaeological finds in Israel is a small ivory pomegranate supposedly from King Solomon's Temple (eighth century BCE) with a written Hebrew inscription on the surface. This thumb-sized artefact became the subject of a lengthy and bitter court case to determine whether it was genuine. The judges concluded that it probably was not.

The pomegranate was one of the three fruits identified as growing in the land of Israel by the spies sent there by Moses. It featured as a design on the hem of the vestments of the high priest of the Temple and depictions of the fruit were also carved into the capitals of the Temple's supporting pillars.

It appeared on the coinage of the Hasmonean dynasty (140–116 BCE), and likewise on coins minted by the Jewish authorities at the time of the Great Revolt (66–70 CE). Even today Israeli currency has an image of the pomegranate on the one-lira coin and the more recent two-shekel coin.

The fruit is mentioned six times in the "Song of Songs, traditionally ascribed to King Solomon. The Talmud interprets this as saying that even the most empty Jew is as full of good deeds as the pomegranate is of seeds.

Some rabbis claim that the fruit has 613 seeds, corresponding to the number of commandments in the Torah, but the fruit actually contains anything between two hundred and fourteen hundred seeds. It nevertheless retains symbolic meaning for observant Jews. Pomegranate juice is, even today, combined with tree sap to produce a special black ink used by religious scribes in Israel.

Jewish sages regarded a dream about pomegranates as a good omen especially considering the development of the dreamer's business – the larger the pomegranate one dreams of, the greater likelihood of future success.

Today the fruit has had something of a renaissance, believed to be one of the new "superfoods" for its high levels of antioxidants. Israeli agriculturalists have developed fourteen different strains of pomegranates, although reputedly the best are supposed to come from the village of Kfar Cana, near Nazareth.

Its residents claim that not only is their fruit

Its residents claim that not only is their fruit the best but also their women have the most beautiful breasts in the country.

the best but also their women have the most beautiful breasts in the country. Nowhere is it mentioned whether or not this is the direct result of eating their particular pomegranates.

To my knowledge, no scientific surveys have taken place to validate their claims either with regard to the quality of the fruit or the superiority of the breasts. I await with curiosity their findings and in particular details of their methodology.

A Quiet Green Revolution

The joy of creation

Open any newspaper today and you will read about "sustainability" and "carbon footprints" – exhorting us to save the world's natural resources and make it a better place to live.

This is not an original idea. As far back as Genesis 2:15 the Bible stated: "God took Adam and put him in the Garden of Eden to cultivate and care for it." This precept, embodying the ethos of protecting nature, was intrinsic to the philosophy of the early pioneers. They established the kibbutz movement, planting roots (literally) for the sophisticated agriculture that exists today.

During the British Mandate, architect Charles Ashbee planned to encircle the Old City of Jeru-

salem with greenery. He envisaged the city silhouetted against this backdrop, and in addition planned a walkway in the ramparts so the view outward would overlook green spaces. Ashbee never realized his dream, however, as Jerusalem grew rapidly and buildings were soon erected in many parts of the city.

With the establishment of the state in 1948 the imperative was to provide urgently needed accommodation for the successive waves of immigrants who reached her shores. Urban areas became densely populated, with people housed in apartment buildings with little access to green spaces.

For the last sixteen years, however, there has

been a quiet green revolution. Thanks to the initiative of the Society for the Protection of Nature, responding to grassroots requests for help, three hundred community gardens have been established in Israel.

Fifty of these are located in and around Jerusalem, coordinated by Amanda Lind. On arrival from Britain at age twenty-one, she went to Kibbutz Magen Michael, and subsequently worked at the magnificent Rothschild Gardens in Zichron Yaakov. From here she was sent to train at Kew Gardens in Richmond, UK, before returning to Israel.

Together we visited some of the gardens. The first, the Zamenhof Garden, is a tiny square surrounded by Jerusalem-stone buildings and the fortified block of the American Consulate. There I saw a miniature ecosystem with birds, butterflies,

"I saw a miniature ecosystem with birds, butterflies, flowers and vegetables." (Cicero)

flowers and vegetables, all overseen by the watchful eyes of a scarecrow. A perfect example of how even the smallest urban plot can be transformed into something magical, where people meet to enjoy a connection with the soil.

A scarecrow overlooks the garden

Next we went to an area adjacent to the Natural History Museum that, seven years ago, was an uncultivated strip of land. Today it is an unbelievably beautiful garden with a profusion of trees, flowers and organic vegetable planting, as well as a composting area tended by locals. When I arrived, forty or so volunteers of all ages were weeding, hoeing, pruning, planting, protecting trees and composting. The team is led by Amnon Herzig, a dedicated enthusiast who has been involved since its inception.

It was especially moving to chat with the gardeners and hear how much this place means to them. It is a community center in every sense of the word. One volunteer told me that it provides an opportunity to relax in her otherwise hectic life. Others spoke of the essential role it has in bringing people of different backgrounds together. The isolated, stressed or those simply seeking to be a part of this tranquil oasis meet, join in the necessary work or sit in the shade chatting and watching small children play. I stayed for two hours and was reluctant to leave and confront once more the hustle and bustle of the city.

The value of such gardens is inestimable. Studies show that an involvement with nature reduces stress and ADHD symptoms and improves cognitive function in youngsters. Their school grades and behavior in general improves. Children experience a sense of wonder at seeing how food grows as, unbelievably, many today still think that it comes in plastic containers from a supermarket.

Each of the fifty gardens is unique. One caters predominantly for elderly Ethiopians who back home were farmers, but on arrival in Israel had little contact with nature. The young generation assimilated through school or the army, but the older generation were isolated, speaking little Hebrew and with few ways of integrating. Their garden resolves this. They grow traditional Ethiopian vegetables such as Gomme d'Acacia and this generates feelings of self-esteem when they can take home such familiar produce to their families.

"He who has a garden and a library wants for nothing."

At all the gardens, volunteers learn about water conservation and composting. They bring their waste food to the compost bank, and before Passover any surplus flour is used to make pita at a communal party. Nothing is wasted. The gardeners aim to follow the principle of Shemittah – a biblical injunction to leave the land fallow for a year, every seventh year. The land is allowed to rest, so volunteers engage in other activities such as making benches and equipment for their gardens from recyclable materials.

It was my mother who instilled a love of gardening in me when I was young and it has been with me ever since. When I married, my husband thought that gardening was something that you paid "a little man" to do. Today, however, he is a changed person and constantly thanks me for introducing him to his passion – the garden. It is not unusual to see him out there at 5:00 A.M. in his Wellingtons, digging away happily. In Britain it is customary for people to take up gardening as a hobby when they retire, provided they can still bend down, but here in Jerusalem we have Amanda, years before retirement, demonstrating boundless enthusiasm and consummate professionalism in all that she does.

The Roman philosopher Cicero wrote: "He who has a garden and a library wants for nothing." With my own love for gardening and writing it is curious to realize that very little has changed over the centuries – they felt then much as we do today!

Sabras

Sabra with fruit

The sabra is the fruit of the prickly-pear cactus, having large thorns on the leaves and many small ones on the fruit. Originally from South America, it was brought to Europe several hundred years ago.

In addition to being a food source, it was adopted as a means of creating boundaries to protect livestock and fence off property for security – the spiky leaves being a deterrent to anyone attempting to enter illegally. When the fruit ripens and dispels its seeds, it releases hundreds of tiny bristles that can cause severe eye damage and skin irritation.

An Israeli village, called Sabarin, near Zichron Yaakov, is named after the plant and is still surrounded by this cactus.

The original Arabic name for the prickly pear is *sabar*, meaning patience or tenacity. It is said that one of the definitions of "patience" in Israel is the time it takes for someone to remove all the tiny bristles from a cactus while wearing boxing gloves.

Eliezer Ben-Yehuda, the driving force behind the revival of Hebrew as an everyday language, named the plant *tzabar*, but the preponderance of Yiddish speakers in the country at the time called it *sabres* and this word has prevailed until today.

At the time of the establishment of Israel, the

The
definition
of "patience"
in Israel is
the time
it takes to
remove all
the bristles
from a
cactus while
wearing
boxing
gloves.

Spiky sabra

population, wanting to get away from the old image of the bearded, defenseless shtetl Jew, began to refer to native-born Israelis as *sabra*s because they were seen to have similar characteristics to the fruit – spiky on the outside but soft and sweet inside. This name is still used to refer to anyone born in Israel.

In recent years, thanks to the research of Israeli agriculturalists, the plant has been modified so that it no longer has thorns either on the leaves or the fruit.

I am not sure that even Israeli brainpower can manage to effect the same transformation on the native-born population. Somehow, the idea of a soft-centered Israeli sabra without spikes seems like a contradiction in terms.

Saving Lives Together

In 1978, four-year-old Eli Beer witnessed horrific carnage when a bus was blown up by terrorists. Years later he was thrown to the ground when a suicide bomber detonated a secondary device intended to mutilate and kill bystanders and first-aiders as they rushed to the scene of an initial bomb attack.

Such traumatic experiences were undoubtedly the impetus that, in 2006, led to him to create United Hatzalah – a rapid response service for anyone needing emergency medical aid. Prior to his involvement there were some localized response groups in Israel but Eli coordinated their activities under the umbrella of United Hatzalah. This organization, initially founded by religious Jews, today comprises over two thousand volunteers from the whole spectrum of Israeli society – men and women, secular and religious, Jews and Arabs.

Each volunteer undergoes a rigorous selection and training process of 180 hours, plus one hundred callouts under supervision and follow-up training every two months. They are on call twenty-four hours a day, seven days a week, 365 days a year. Jews can be called out on Shabbat or Yom Kippur and Arabs on their holy days.

Volunteers are equipped with a GPS smartphone and app that automatically contacts whoever is closest to an incident when it occurs. They immediately stop whatever they are doing and race to help. The average arrival time is less than three minutes – a world record for this type of ser-

> "We save
> lives together,
> hand in hand,
> because
> when a life
> is in danger
> differences
> cease to exist."

Ready to go. Well, almost!

vice, achieved by using medically equipped motorcycles that negotiate congested streets rapidly.

Israel's major provider of emergency medical aid is Magen Dovid Adom – the Red Star of David, recognized as Israel's national emergency service in 1950. Their ambulances operate nationwide, staffed mainly by volunteers. Recently, however, sectarian violence in Arab villages near Jerusalem led to some local residents throwing stones and Molotov cocktails at the ambulances when they arrived in the villages to help.

As a result, police escorts must now accompany them to ensure safe passage, but the extra time this involves puts lives at risk – the speed with which aid reaches a patient often being the determining factor between life and death.

This is where Hatzalah provides a crucial additional service. Its volunteers give emergency treatment until an MDA ambulance arrives to take patients to hospital.

I was intrigued to know what makes these volunteers tick. I visited their central command in Jerusalem where they took calls and focused intently on an array of sophisticated computer screens. There was an atmosphere of calm efficiency and alert attention.

This center is hardwired to the IDF (Israel Defense Forces) in the event of any attack on the home front. Should the center itself be attacked, a backup set of everything needed to function is kept in an underground room so that their work can continue unimpeded.

A storeroom is piled high with equipment, manned by three Haredi (ultra-religious) volunteers who work there fulltime instead of doing army service.

They insisted that I don a full set of combat equipment – bulletproof jacket (fifteen pounds) and helmet to match and also a twenty-two-pound pack of equipment. It was extremely heavy and I wondered about the Amazonian proportions of any women volunteers who could possibly enter the fray wearing such gear.

The dedication of the people I met was impressive, and I asked what motivated them to volunteer. They explained that it was a matter of putting others before oneself, minimizing one's ego and following the precept in the Torah to strive "to be of benefit to others." The payback for the volunteer is the tremendous feel-good factor when saving a life. This, I was told, becomes addictive. But as addictions go, this one seems to be pretty high up in the scale of social values.

Jewish law states: "Whoever saves a single life is considered as if he had saved the entire world" (Mishnah *Sanhedrin* 4:5). This is repeated in the Koran. It is heartwarming to see this principle being upheld today by members of both religions through the work of Hatzalah, whose mission is "We save lives together, hand in hand, because when a life is in danger differences cease to exist."

Volunteer on duty

> Balsam was the most valuable commodity in the world — its resin sold by weight at a price equal to twice that of gold.

Scents of History

Cutting balsam, Ein Gedi, 2014

Unlike most women I have never really understood the attraction of perfume. As a teenager I would receive occasional gifts from admirers but they were invariably ill chosen. One, called "Poison," advertised as Dior's ultimate weapon of seduction, was in my case the ultimate cause of nausea. It ended up in the drawer reserved for unwanted tributes, waiting to be taken to the charity store.

Imagine, therefore, my slight trepidation at the prospect of writing a story about scent, as while researching *Unexpected Israel* I discovered that Ein Gedi, the oasis on the edge of the Dead Sea, was at one time the main production center for a perfume called Balsam.

But this was no common or garden perfume, rather something totally unique and exceptional. According to the Jewish historian Flavius Josephus, the Queen of Sheba brought the first balsam bushes to Judea for King Solomon around three thousand years ago. This was a gift of outstanding generosity, for balsam was then the most valuable commodity in the world. Its resin sold by weight at a price equal to twice that of gold. Consequently it became an important part of royal revenue.

It was so highly regarded that Theophrastus (a student of Aristotle, fourth to third century BCE), the first non-Jew to write about Judaism, which he considered a model philosophical religion, wrote nothing of the Jewish homeland except about

> The cultivators of balsam belonged to a guild that survived for over a thousand years.

balsam. Two centuries later the Greek historian, Diodorus Siculus, wrote extensively about it, describing among other things the importance of Judean balsam as a successful treatment for a wide range of ailments.

In Roman times, Mark Anthony took the balsam plantations away from their owner, King Herod, and presented them to his lover Cleopatra – a gift unmatched by anything known in the ancient world.

Later, in 68 CE during the First Jewish Revolt, Roman forces largely destroyed Ein Gedi but balsam production continued, with the Jews toiling under the yoke of their oppressors. Pliny the Elder wrote of this, elaborating on the highly complex process of extracting resin from the bushes, which was carried out under the strictest secrecy.

So esteemed was this perfume that Emperor Vespasian and his son Titus ordered a balsam bush to be displayed during their triumphal procession through Rome. This was one of their affirmations of power, demonstrating that these bushes were now the property of the Roman Empire. A depiction of this can be seen on the Arch of Titus in Rome, commemorating the destruction of the Temple and the capture of Judea.

More recently archaeological finds have confirmed balsam's importance. In 1965 a mosaic synagogue floor from the Byzantine period was uncovered at Ein Gedi. It bore an inscription counseling the community to keep their "secrets" and cursing anyone who might reveal them. Archaeologists consider that this referred to the closely guarded details of balsam production. In addition, evidence of perfume manufacture was discovered at nearby Arugot.

The cultivators of balsam belonged to a guild that, amazingly, survived for over a thousand years. It was not until around the sixth century CE that Ein Gedi was once more destroyed, this time by the Bedouin, and balsam cultivation ceased. Since then many attempts have been made to recreate this enigmatic perfume.

In 1998, excavations at Qumran conducted by the Hebrew University and the Texan archaeologist Wendell Jones (supposedly the inspiration for the movie character Indiana Jones) unearthed a first-century CE clay jug containing dark, sticky oil. Jones claimed it was the long-lost perfume, but extensive analysis failed to confirm its botanical identity.

To bring the story up to date I visited Ein Gedi where I met Mani Gal, a botanist. He told me that in 2003 seeds were brought from England by Professor Zohar Amar and planted at Ein Gedi, where they have now grown into bushes of about five feet high.

We entered a locked compound, where dense prickly bushes with tiny leaves and small berries were growing on terraces. At once I noticed an unusual and pervasive scent.

Mani explained how Professor Amar considered that ancient balsam is probably one of the species of myrrh (Commiphora Gileadensis). The factors that convinced him are that the scent of the resin is carried in the air. Additionally, this resin is also flammable, and when the sap is put into a sealed bottle it does not solidify.

Mani took out a small, sharp object and gently scored a stem. Immediately, a white sap seeped out. It was unbelievably sticky and smelled strong, unusual and quite unlike anything I have ever come across. I asked if we were any closer to discovering the secrets of balsam. He replied that the kibbutz itself does not have the resources to engage in research but that scientists are using the plantation to work on different aspects of this elusive plant, including its medical uses.

Today, a flourishing perfume trade exists in Israel claiming to use "aromatic essences" from over ninety plants, including frankincense, myrrh and spikenard. "Scents of the Bible" are sold in hand-painted bottles "inspired by" those found at archaeological sites. Products are advertised as essences for industry, detergents, air fresheners and wet wipes. For me, sadly, this link with toilet deodorizers fails utterly to conjure up the allure of a perfume once associated with the Queen of Sheba and Cleopatra.

Israeli manufacturers do nevertheless manage to capture the imagination when naming their products, offering "King David," "King Solomon" and "Lion of Judah" aftershave, as well as "Queen of Sheba" anointing oil and, surprisingly, one named "Ruth" – the perfect gift for me, I suppose, if only I knew who, what, when or how to anoint.

So will we ever again experience the fabulous balsam? Under the guidance of Professor Amar, botanists believe they have once again restored balsam to Ein Gedi, connecting us with the Jews of ancient times. We can only hold our breath

Its pungent odor was one of the methods used by the sinful daughters of Zion to entice lovers.

and wait, but imagine the excitement if they do succeed and we might once again breathe in the aroma that so captivated our ancestors.

However I am not quite sure how our rabbis will react. Balsam is mentioned in the Talmud and a special blessing for it exists, so we are prepared in this respect. But the Midrash goes on to describe "its pungent odor" as one of the methods used by the sinful daughters of Zion to entice lovers (*Lamentations Rabbah* 4:18). Do I sense a slight whiff of disapproval?

On reflection I have decided that the final word must go to those rabbis who teach us that "in messianic times the righteous will bathe in thirteen rivers of balsam" (Jerusalem Talmud, *Av. Zar.* 3:1, 42). Now *that* is something to look forward to!

Sheshbesh (Backgammon)

Players at Mahane Yehuda, Jerusalem

Sheshbesh is a national pastime in Israel.

Arab shop owners sit with their friends in the Old City of Jerusalem enjoying a game, as do Tel Avivians on the beach and in Hayarkon Park. *Sheshbesh* is also the game of choice among army reservists on their annual duty when they have free time.

There is one special place, however, that has been home to many devotees for around sixty years. It is located in the Iraqi Shuk – a small square tucked away in a corner of the Mahane Yehuda market in Jerusalem. Every day up to one hundred men come to meet their friends and play.

They come rain or shine. In the winter there are club rooms adjacent to the square where they also play card games, but only men may enter. Once I tried to go in to take pictures and was gently ushered outside.

In the summer months they sit outside ignoring curious passersby and concentrating on winning. Money changes hands rapidly, but it is the game itself and the companionship that draws them together. The men, mostly retired, generally stay all day with a short break for lunch. This is where they catch up on news, gossip with friends, test their skill and win a few games. These continue nonstop, with lots of banter and coins changing hands at a rate of knots.

It is evident that they cherish their little, exclusive corner of the world. One player told me, "I would really love to die here playing *sheshbesh* – it would be a wonderful way to go."

When I tried to take photographs one stopped me: "Please!" he said, covering his face with his hands. "I don't want my wife to know where I am all day!" She is probably delighted to have him out from under her feet and engaged in what is, in fact, a relatively harmless activity.

They play with lots of banter and coins changing hands at a rate of knots.

The men's gaming club. Iraqi shuk, Mahane Yehuda

Shikmah trees were so highly prized that King David appointed a special overseer to care for them.

The *Shikmah* (Sycamore Fig Tree)

Alon standing by the trunk of "his" shikmah

Trees have always had a very important place in the life of Israel. As a Jewish child growing up in Britain, I remember how whenever there was an occasion to celebrate, families would purchase "tree certificates" so that trees would be planted in their name in Israel. I am still waiting for the day when I may find one of them with my name on it!

This recognition of the need to plant trees goes back to Talmudic times when it was specified that for every boy born, the family should plant a tree to provide wood to build his future home. For a girl it was prescribed that the tree must be a *shikmah* (sycamore fig), from which to make furniture when she reached adulthood.

The *shikmah* originated in Africa and Egypt, where its wood was highly valued for use in building work and the construction of coffins. It was highly suitable for this purpose as the wood did not absorb damp and therefore would not rot.

It was probably imported into Israel during the early biblical period and was so highly prized by King David that he appointed a special overseer to take responsibility for these trees, which at that time grew prolifically in Israel.

My connection with the *shikmah* was through my friend Alon.

In 1968 the Ministry of Transport decided to construct a new road in the north of the country. Directly in the path of their proposed route stood a group of four huge, ancient *shikmah* trees that the engineers intended to uproot and destroy. The Parks Authority, for which Alon worked at the time, fought this plan fiercely and eventually reached a compromise that the trees must be carefully lifted and moved to a safer resting place.

This proposal was put into action. All the top branches of the trees were trimmed, and the enormous roots were hauled up by a massive crane and loaded onto trucks to move them to another location. This complex engineering process took over a week and then began the work of caring for the trees to ensure they settled into their new home.

Alon and I visited two of these trees near the border with Lebanon. There they stood, descendants of years of tradition. We checked the cir-

cumference of one trunk and it measured more than thirty feet around the base, not much bigger than when he had moved it so many years ago.

I told Alon that coming here must be like visiting one of his children – to which he replied that he had many such children in Israel from his years with the Parks Authority. A wonderful legacy for someone to leave behind!

Coincidentally the Hebrew root of the word *shikmah* means to restore, regenerate and reestablish, which happily was the end result of this exercise.

> The trunk measured more than thirty feet around the base.

Figs growing from the shikmah *tree trunk*

From Sickness to Health

Hansen Hospital today, night scene

In 2012 I was invited to give a lecture at the Jewish Museum in London on the history of photography in Israel.

Months of research led me down some unexpected pathways, not the least being the discovery of the Matson Collection of photographs comprising twenty-two thousand images taken by successive American and Swedish missionaries in Jerusalem from 1898 to 1934.

One photograph, under the classification "Costumes and Characters," was quite disturbing. Called "Lepers in Jerusalem" it was not so much the image that bothered me as the text that

accompanied it: "Here for your enjoyment is an exciting picture of lepers."

At first I was shocked, but then I recalled that in those days it was not unusual for fairground owners to exhibit "freaks of nature" – people or animals with severe and unusual medical or physical conditions. Many were faked, but nevertheless they attracted huge crowds – an activity unacceptable by today's politically correct standards.

On my last visit to Jerusalem I discovered that in 1897 in a leafy suburb of the city, German Protestants established the Hansen Hospital specifically to treat lepers. Conrad Schick, a German missionary and self-taught architect, designed a

"Here
for your
enjoyment
is an
exciting
picture of
lepers."

magnificent building comprising a two-story bal-conied structure with terraced gardens, trees and water cisterns. It was an open institution where visitors could enter freely and patients were able to leave at will. The original European caregiv-ers advocated a regime of fresh air, good food and physical exercise as well as support for the soul administered by members of the Moravian Church. They grew their own food and kept live-stock so as to be self-sufficient.

The term "leprosy" features sixty times in the Bible, where it refers to a number of different skin conditions but not leprosy as we know it today. This was confirmed, in the twelfth century, by the leading Sephardic rabbi, philosopher and physi-cian Maimonides.

It was believed that the condition was inflicted as divine punishment for the sins of those affected. The "leper," after being examined by priests, was then cast out of society. These abandoned crea-tures were undoubtedly also expelled through fears that their condition was contagious.

Today we know, thanks to research in the 1870s by Gerhard Hansen, a Norwegian, that leprosy is one of the least infectious bacterial diseases, easily cured by modern drugs. Hansen had even tried to infect himself with the bacillus but failed.

I was fortunate to meet Ruth Wexler, the nurse who had worked at the hospital since 1988 when the building became the responsibility of the Israel Health Ministry. When she began there were about twenty-five patients, mostly new-comers from the 1950s. Surprisingly the hospital closed only as recently as 2000, but Ruth con-tinues to work in this field at Hadassah Hospi-tal – treating a few new patients each year, mostly foreign workers and immigrants.

Happily, this splendid historic building that once housed and cared for patients has been con-verted into an arts and music center. A small mu-seum devoted to its history remains. I wandered around during the renovations – it is a wonder-fully atmospheric building with many corners in the extensive gardens where you can sit, relax and enjoy the sights and sounds of nature. It is not difficult to imagine how life must have been for the residents in such an oasis of calm.

As for the future, it is edifying to know that a place that once served to cure the sick will now feed the soul and raise the spirits of those who come to enjoy the variety of cultural activities on offer. An example of how a "leprosarium" once regarded with fear and ignorance can, with a bit of imagination, be transformed into something positive and creative.

Thanks to
Gerhard
Hansen, a
Norwegian,
we now
know that
leprosy
is easily
treated by
antibiotics.

Snow

Snow is something not immediately associated with a hot Mediterranean country like Israel. It does fall in the north on Mount Hermon, but rarely in the center of the country. When it does, however, the effect on the population is dramatic. It only needs a few wisps to fall for all the residents of Jerusalem to move immediately into panic mode.

All places of work are vacated – schools, stores and government offices emptied. People rush immediately to the supermarket to buy "emergency" provisions and then hurry home in a frenzy of anxiety that they might (God forbid) be snowbound. This rarely happens as the few flakes that

manage to fall hardly settle on the ground long enough to justify being called snow.

But not only Jerusalemites are affected. Once snow is reported thousands of people living on the coastal plain make evacuation plans, but this time to go and visit the snow. It is probably one of the rare occasions when Tel Avivians deign to visit the capital city.

To travel by car is an ordeal – not because of harsh weather conditions, but because of the tremendous traffic jams caused by others who have the same idea. One TA friend rented a 4×4 in order to take the back route over small mountain tracks rather than risk the congestion on the main highway.

However, Tel Avivians have found an ingenious way to combat this. They call a friend in Jerusalem and ask him to fill his car trunk with snow and to meet them halfway on the main highway at Latrun. Here it is transferred from car to car and the Tel Avivians return home exultant with their hoard. I have yet to discover if any of it actually reaches its destination. I guess that, sadly, all he has when he reaches home is a rather damp patch in the trunk of the car.

But never mind, it is said that in life the journey is more important than the arrival. In this case, for a brief period the excitement of the adventure takes thoughts away from some of the more pressing issues that affect Israelis.

Shoveling snow into the car

Snowman

It is probably one of the rare occasions when Tel Avivians deign to visit the capital city.

Soup of Human Kindness

Illegal immigrants on the streets of Tel Aviv

Etti is a potter who lives and works in one of the poorer parts of south Tel Aviv. Not far from her home is the area where, since 2005, fifty-thousand illegal immigrants have arrived seeking refuge, from countries such as southern Sudan and Eritrea.

Most entered Israel illegally from the Sinai in Egypt, "helped" along their way by Bedouin tribesmen who took the opportunity to profit with promises of safe passage across the Israeli border.

Sadly this has not always been the case. Instead, there have been well-documented stories of migrants being killed and their organs taken for transplants, of others being kidnapped for ransom. In addition there have been many, many incidences reported of women being tortured and raped.

Etti saw these newcomers and heard about their heartbreaking stories and the trials they endured en route to Israel. At a women's refuge she came face-to-face with many of the young girls

"As a human being I could not stand by and ignore this."

Photo: Misha Vallejo.
Courtesy of Etti Goren.

Toddler at the kindergarten, Tel Aviv

who arrived in Israel pregnant, terrified and lonely. Israeli voluntary groups have been established to help these casualties of displacement but they cannot heal their scars.

Etti was so moved by their plight. "As a human being I could not stand by and ignore this," she said. With limited financial resources, she sought to do something using her skills as a potter and capitalizing on the kindness of her many friends from the world of ceramics. She galvanized them into action, asking them to produce soup bowls. These were taken to the Jos and Loz Restaurant, where the chef made soup, filled the bowls and sold them to well-wishers to raise money.

Etti's next project was to find money to fix the roof of a kindergarten for migrants' children, where one man and three women look after forty-four babies, from infants to four year olds. They barely have time to do much for the infants other than to feed and change them but at least they are well cared for while their mothers try to find work.

Happily enough, money was raised to fix the roof and in addition provide much needed items for the little ones. Visitors brought toys, stayed to play with the children and enjoyed a cup of Eritrean coffee.

The influx of so many arriving in a small country like Israel (the same size as Wales) has many implications for its future and ultimately can only be resolved by political means. However, "Love thy neighbor as thyself" is a precept that goes back to the Bible.

What these potters have done in extending the hand of friendship to these people in need is fundamental to Jewish thought and practice. They have created something through their passion and skill and in doing so made a tangible difference to the lives of others.

Sport for Peace

It was my good friend the late John Harlow who, after reading my stories, asked whether there were any instances of sport bringing people together in Israel, much like that extraordinary time in 1914, during World War 1, when British and German troops ceased hostilities and joined together to play football and exchange gifts at Christmas.

This started me thinking, for in my mind the word *football* conjures up images not of peace and goodwill, but of senseless football hooliganism.

Having been born in Manchester this should not really be my reaction. I was there on that unforgettable day when the plane crashed in Munich in 1958, killing half our Manchester United team. I grieved along with everyone else in the city. As a Mancunian I have been privileged to bask in the reflected glory both of the team and

the even more glorious David Beckham. On holidays abroad, to places as remote as the Atacama Desert, or isolated villages in India and Vietnam, the mere mention of Manchester results in howls of delight from young men insisting on shaking my hand simply because of where I was born. It is a badge of honor and an immediate passport to popularity.

The origins of football violence in England date back to 1314 when the game involved kicking a pig's bladder across a patch of ground. King Edward II banned the sport, fearing that it could lead to social unrest. How prescient he was, for throughout history there have been thousands of incidences involving clashes between rival fans, and many "supporters" attend the match as much for the "punch up" as for the game itself.

Today's UK fans are known as "firms," such as the Norwich Hit Squad, Stoke City's Naughty Forty, Swindon's Aggro Boys and Tottenham Hotspur's Yid's Army. No country in the world is free from this scourge of aggressive displays by some supporters, including Betar in Israel.

So how can such an apparently socially divisive activity be turned into something for good?

I found the answer at the Peres Center for Peace in Tel Aviv, where young people are encouraged to be actively engaged in peace building through sport. Fifteen thousand youths have been "making friends through soccer" since 1996. Teams from schools with different ethnic backgrounds practice independently, meeting at a monthly sports camp where they mix both on and off the pitch. Many arrive with negative impressions of "the other" but after a weekend of fun together they part as friends. It works.

In 2014 the Brits got involved. Co-existence Through Football, an initiative of the British embassy and the Football Association, arranges for UK coaches to train disadvantaged Arab and Jewish youngsters. They will work with around two thousand of them over the next couple of years. When it comes to the question of what to wear, I wonder which team gets the Gaza strip?

As for cricket, that quintessential British sport, the Peres Center, the Israel Cricket Association and the Al-Quds Association for Democracy and Dialogue launched their Cricket 4 Peace initiative with considerable success.

Coincidentally, in 1951 my husband Charles played in the first cricket match in Israel after the establishment of the state. Before starting, the teams had to clear debris off the "pitch" and as the game reached an exciting climax, the umpire abandoned the match. Not because "rain stopped play" or "fading light," but because it was Friday and Shabbat was approaching.

Eleven years ago Freddie Krivine established tennis clubs for Arab and Jewish children. Some

have excelled and won scholarships to study in the United States and others have become professional tennis coaches, working with children in Israel.

My personal experience of "sport for peace" occurred in 1973 while living in Sunderland. This was the momentous year when Sunderland won the FA Cup at Wembley. Half a million people lined the streets to welcome home "wor lads." I was commissioned to write a piece about the effects of this win and can tell you that for a few days the atmosphere of the city totally changed. People were nice to each other and the town became an undivided community bound together by the magical feet of eleven men.

Thousands flooded into Roker Park Football Ground to pay tribute to their team. An endless but orderly line snaked around the park. I could not imagine what so many people had come to see, but there, raised on a dais was *the* boot of *the* player, Ian Porterfield, who had scored the winning goal. It was plated in gold.

Forget your golden calf, this was idol worship at its most potent as crowds filed silently past to pay their respects. But this was no one-day phenomenon. In 2007 Porterfield died. At the funeral his golden boot was placed on the altar, giving the faithful yet another opportunity to reconfirm their allegiance.

As Liverpool manager Bill Shankly once declared, "Football is not just a matter of life and death – it is much more serious."

The umpire abandoned the cricket match, not because "rain stopped play" but because Shabbat was approaching.

Standing on Line

It looks like a bus line in Jerusalem but …

The comedian Jackie Mason first brought to my attention the fact that Jews don't stand in line. Imagine, then, how this translates into a whole country where most of the population is Jewish.

Occasionally a line may begin, but after three or so people have hovered together, the waiting area becomes chaotic with lines going haphazardly in different directions and people walking to the front, with the pretense of talking to friends or ostensibly to ask a question, more often to remain there.

I was told a wonderful story about what happened to a friend of a friend. She lived in Moscow and when it became permissible to emigrate to Israel, she went to the Department for Visa Reg-

istration. There she encountered a very long line. She moved around trying to look unobtrusive while wondering how to edge forward without making her intentions too obvious. After a while the man who was standing in front of her turned and said in a tired voice, "Excuse me, but surely by now you realize that we are all Jews here so you are really wasting your time."

Trying to stand in line in Israel is a challenge, particularly should you need the ladies room in a shopping mall at holiday time. Talk about "hell breaking loose" – the experience is probably not too different to how it will actually be in the next world down under. Others push in front but you must stand your ground and learn to "talk" with your elbows. Any rebuke to "intruders" is met with a shrug of the shoulders meaning anything from "So what!" to "Hard luck!"

Some Israeli organizations – the post office, IKEA and banks – try to encourage a more orderly system. On entering their premises, you take a ticket from a machine and then wait, impatiently, for your number to be called.

I am amazed that no enterprising Israeli has realized the commercial potential of this. Surely if one went in very early and took a quantity of tickets, it would not be impossible to convert these into hard cash by offering tickets to those wanting an earlier number than they are holding. Price could be negotiable, dependent on the number of people waiting on line, their desperation to get out quickly and their willingness to pay for the privilege.

Sometimes I get nostalgic for the way we do

"Jews don't stand in line."
– Jackie Mason

things in the United Kingdom. Britain has a long and established tradition of disciplined standing in line, perfected over years of practice.

When Apple launched their new iPlayer in London, the line stretched for three blocks. Many of those waiting were sent by their bosses, who paid them to wait to ensure they would be the first to get one of the "whatever it is latest must-have adult toy."

A new occupation is emerging. Now it is not enough to have a chauffeur, nanny, gardener, personal fitness trainer, life coach, hairdresser or manicurist – today's executive needs to have their own "gentleman in waiting."

Now that is how things should be done!

More standing on line, Jerusalem style

The Story of the Disappearing Carrot

For years I lived in the north of England, bastion of the working class, where recreational activities of the local males were:

1. Beating up the wife on Friday night when the pubs closed.
2. "Ferret legging" which involved placing a ferret in your pants for as long as possible while the animal nibbled sensitive parts of your anatomy – the world record being five hours and thirty minutes.

3. Growing the largest leeks possible – achieved by urinating (leaking) on them frequently. Growing giant vegetables was a gentle pastime for gentlemen, but often beset with drama and intrigue, competitors frequently sneaking out at night to slash and destroy their rivals' leeks.

Coming from this background, it was hardly surprising that I became so excited on hearing that Kibbutz Dorot in Israel was growing carrots weighing fifteen pounds or more each. I simply had to see these for myself.

Dorot, one of the largest growers of carrots in Israel, has nearly four thousand acres using massive tractors and ultra-sophisticated machinery. Far removed from my imagined idyll of a simple rural cooperative. I was welcomed by their manager who told me how they export to Russia, Mexico, Europe and the west coast of the United States. Carrots do actually grow in California, but apparently road transport across the States costs more than freighting by ship from Israel.

Becoming impatient, I asked if I could please see the extra large carrots I had heard so much about. He gave me a bemused look. They grow, he said, to a maximum of around twelve inches with a diameter of two inches.

I hoped my disappointment was not too evident as the realization dawned on me that the story about these king carrots was turning out to be nothing more than an urban myth – or perhaps in this case a rural myth. The story grew less interesting by the second.

The manager, perhaps sensing my letdown, proceeded to tell me how Dorot, the largest growers of garlic in Israel, are engaged in groundbreaking work with scientists at the Weizmann Institute, producing garlic capsules that don't dissolve in stomach acids but are effectively absorbed into the body, thereby reducing blood pressure and high cholesterol.

Well, it was all very impressive, but sadly not the fifteen-pound carrot I had come to see.

Back in London, however, I discovered to my supreme joy, that the world's *longest* carrot, measuring a magnificent nineteen feet two inches, is British! It was somehow appropriate that I became aware of this during the Queen's jubilee celebrations, giving me yet another reason to demonstrate my national pride.

After much reflection, however, I decided to consign this esoteric piece of information to my collection of miscellanea on English eccentricity. Incidentally, for those of you who still remain interested, International Carrot Day is April 4 each year.

Now here's a turn up for the book!

So what has all this got to do with Israel you might well ask. Well, unbeknown to me, my friend and guide Alon had dedicated himself to try to find some of these monster carrots.

Six months after this story was completed he sent me a set of images of king carrots. OK, they may not be exactly fifteen pounds, perhaps only seven or eight, but they are definitely getting bigger and are very impressive. Who knows, by the time this book is published we might even get close to our original estimate, especially as recently the world's heaviest carrot clocked in, again in Britain, at an astonishing twenty pounds courtesy of a Mr. Peter Glazebrook. Who knows what the future will hold?

Impressive or what!

Succoth (The Feast of Tabernacles)

Succoth is one of the major Jewish festivals and takes place in the autumn. It is a reminder of the days when the Israelites traveled in the wilderness and had to live in temporary dwellings after their exodus from Egypt. It is also thanksgiving for a bountiful harvest.

All over the world Jews build temporary booths in which they eat meals, entertain friends and in some cases even sleep for eight days. The walls can be built of any material but the roof must be of organic matter – we use palm fronds – with enough

gaps for the stars to be seen. Constructing these dwellings, for a people not renowned for their DIY expertise, is something of an annual challenge. In Jerusalem, where people are mainly apartment dwellers, it becomes even more so. One can see imaginative and precariously built structures protruding from balconies all over the city.

As well as building the booth (succah), other rituals are observed. Four species of plants are purchased: a citron, a palm frond, three myrtle twigs and two willow branches. These have sym-

Inspecting the myrtle and the lulav

bolic significance. Buying these items is a far from simple matter.

In the run-up to the festival stalls are set up where black-hatted men congregate, armed with tape measure and magnifying glass, to inspect each item closely to ensure it is as near perfect as possible. Once this rigorous examination is exhausted, buyers can take their purchases home and on the festival say the requisite blessings and shake them with confidence (shaking being part of the ritual).

The original commandment to build and live in these dwellings was written with Israel in mind, where the weather is usually clement. Nothing was written about what to do if you live in northern Europe or America or indeed anywhere else where *warmth* and *October* are not synonymous.

With the onset of freezing rain and howling winds rabbis permit the use of electric heaters, but there is another escape clause. Strictly speaking, one must stay in the succah even though it is raining. The only time you can ignore this, and race indoors, is if, God forbid, the rain should fall into and spoil your soup.

Who but the Jews would have special laws to protect their food! There is nothing like having a good set of priorities.

One must stay in the succah even though it rains — unless the rain spoils your soup.

Choosing an etrog

> "The trick is to leave politics and religion at the door — once we are in the gym we are all brothers with a common bond."

The Sweet Science of Boxing

Yefim, seventy years old, a veteran boxer

Boxing reminds me immediately of my late father. He loved it and whenever there was a match on TV he would be glued to the screen and sit there throwing punches at an imagined adversary. He would get so excited that my mother usually had to turn it off in case he suffered a heart attack! How he would have loved this story.

At a time of so much media coverage of the tension between Arabs and Jews in Israel, a beacon of light shines in the most unlikely of places – a cramped, converted underground bomb shelter in a working-class area of Jerusalem. This is where you will find Israel's only official boxing club, established thirty-four years ago by the Luxemburg brothers, Gershon and Eli.

Born in Tashkent, Uzbekistan, the brothers began boxing at a young age to protect themselves from anti-Semitic attacks. They developed such proficiency that Eli became the Soviet champion and Gershon the champion of Uzbekistan and then seven-times Israeli champion.

Gershon immigrated to Israel in 1972, at age twenty-eight, and served in the army during two wars. In 1981 he decided to follow his dream and set up a club to train young players to compete in national and international boxing events.

The club opened to everyone and aspiring boxers came from all levels of society – Jews and Arabs, men and women, religious and secular – a mix rarely seen in the outside world. Many of his pupils were successful at events including the Olympics, the Maccabiah and the European championships. However Gershon gradually realized that he was not only teaching a sport, but also creating a second home and a socially cohesive environment for people of diverse backgrounds.

In spite of the violent reputation of the sport, he has never once seen a clash between Jews and Arabs in the gym. One thirty-seven-year-old Palestinian said, "The trick is to leave politics and religion at the door – once we are in the gym we are all brothers with a common bond."

It was time for me to pay a visit and see the club for myself. I went with my taxi-driver friend Gaby, also originally from Uzbekistan. He was delighted to come as, unbeknown to me, he knew Gershon really well, having trained with him thirty years ago.

Descending the steps into the shelter we were immediately confronted by a large portrait of Muhammad Ali, surrounded by thousands more photographs of boxers covering every inch of the walls.

The "trainees" began to arrive – maybe thirty or more, ages seven to seventy. As each one entered, the first thing they did was to shake Gershon's hand or give him a big hug. It was like a family get-together with him as the benevolent father figure.

Next, training began – circuit after circuit round the perimeter of the two rooms – running, skipping, hopping, carrying one another – an endless succession of fitness exercises that exhausted me just watching. This "warm-up" continued for an hour. They then paired off, wearing protective gear, to practice sparring or attacking punch bags with determination.

For me it was an occasion for reflection. I had always recoiled from boxing, regarding it as a gory exercise in testosterone-fueled aggression.

However to my great surprise, I began to see it in a different light – as creative, skillful and almost balletic. Apparently those who really understand boxing know that while it can be brutal, it also combines finesse and strategy. The way the fighters dance to avoid being hit, while simultaneously planning one move ahead of their adversaries, is a true art form.

I never knew until I began researching this story that boxing is known as "the sweet science." This phrase, coined in 1813 by British sportswriter Pierce Egan, described boxers as tough, forward thinking and tactical. Lennox Lewis said, "In boxing you create a strategy to beat each new opponent, just like chess" and it was said that Sugar Ray Robinson, who received his nickname from "the

Laura from the United States, at home in the gym

"I don't care if they become boxing champions, so long as they become champions in life."

sweet science," boxed as though he were playing a violin.

Interestingly, the father of scientific boxing was Daniel Mendoza, a Jew who became the first Jewish prizefighter to win the UK championship from 1792 to 1795. At that time fighting was with bare knuckles, but Mendoza, being only five feet seven inches and 160 pounds, developed strategies to help him win against much larger heavyweights. His techniques included sidestepping, ducking, blocking and in general avoiding being hit. His book *The Art of Boxing* became the bible for every subsequent boxer. Mendoza also helped to transform the stereotype of the weak and defenseless Jew into someone who won respect and he is supposedly the first Jew ever to talk to King George III.

A second UK boxer, closer to home, is a distant cousin of my husband. In his youth he was a boxer called "Fat Moishe" and "Cockney Cohen." He was also a petty thief, being trained by a crook called "Harry the Ganof" (Yiddish for *thief*). In spite of this, or perhaps because of it, he rose to fame as "Two-Gun Cohen" and eventually became the aide-de-camp of Sun Yat Sen and embarked on an illustrious international career.

These are just two examples of how boys from poor backgrounds could, through boxing, rise through the ranks and elevate their status.

This dualism combining strength and skill intrigued me, and was something I identified in Gershon's personality. He is not interested in just teaching kids how to throw punches – instead he wants them to grow to respect themselves and others, regardless of their background. "I don't care if they become boxing champions, so long as they become champions in life."

He says: "I take an ordinary stone from the ground, clean it, polish it, care for it, and it becomes a beautiful piece of sculpture." Gershon has soul, integrity and sensitivity, so it was almost no

> I take an ordinary stone from the ground, clean it, polish it, care for it, and it becomes a beautiful sculpture."

surprise to discover that he has had three books published – not on boxing, but on poetry.

This extraordinary man is on a mission. He has a day job as a security guard, but several times a week he runs the gym, without recompense, giving of himself to everyone who comes. His satisfaction is evident. Youngsters arrive at the club for the first time, angry, aggressive, often from poor or broken homes. With Gershon's guidance they develop confidence and the realization that they no longer need to look for battles.

My time there reminded me once again not to be judgmental, particularly about things I know little of. This is the first and only boxing club I have ever entered and I was astonished to see a prayer in Hebrew pinned to the wall. It is a request to the Almighty for peace together with a strong and healthy body and concludes with quotations from the Prophets.

I wondered if this is was common practice, and, after investigating further, I found another prayer, this time from a Bishop Kelly in Ireland. The content is virtually the same and I found it touching to realize that this ethos is intrinsic in a sport that originally I had rejected as more than somewhat barbaric!

> I ask you not for victory…for
> somehow, that seems wrong,
> But only for protection and
> the courage to be strong.
> Strength – not to conquer, but
> just that I'll fight well
> And prove myself a sports-
> man at the final bell.

Swift's Return

Mayor Nir Barkat welcoming the swifts back to Jerusalem

In early March 2012 a special ceremony took place at the Western Wall in Jerusalem signifying the arrival of spring.

What, you might ask, are the religious aspects of this? Absolutely none whatsoever.

The only reason for this event was to celebrate the return of the common swift, a small bird that spends most of its time flying – so much so that it can feed (by catching flying insects), mate and even sleep while on the wing. It drinks by swooping down and taking water into its mouth while still in flight.

The swift spends most of the year in South Africa. Each spring it flies north, the migratory path passing through Israel until it arrives at one of its first breeding sites in Jerusalem. Ever since man began constructing cities, the swift has become dependent on humans, choosing to locate its nests in high places. It is unable to walk as other birds do, but has claws with which it clings to cliffs and walls. It cannot take flight from ground level, which is why it locates its nests in high buildings including many holy sites such as churches, mosques and in this case, the Western Wall.

Swifts are monogamous; they choose a partner for life and after building their nest, return to the same one every year. After the eggs hatch and the fledgling chicks have grown, they return to Africa in early June.

It was the prophet Jeremiah who pointed out how migrating birds knew instinctively when to travel north or south, whereas people did not have any moral compass. To try to validate his observations, researchers recorded, over several years, the dates upon which the birds arrived. Jeremiah was right. It was proven that they come at the same time each year, give or take a few days. In 2002 researchers also recorded that eighty-eight swifts' nests were located in the Western Wall. So important are these to Israeli nature conservationists that during the process of strengthening the Wall, the nests were left unharmed.

In March 2012 I was invited by the Friends of the Swifts Association, part of the Society for the Protection of Nature in Israel, to a special ceremony at the Western Wall. A couple of hundred enthusiastic bird supporters and some school groups attended and heard Mayor Nir Barkat speak of these birds as symbolic pilgrims regularly returning to their nesting places in Jerusalem.

Sitting there at the onset of dusk and watching these astonishing creatures whirling and flitting across the darkening skies, hearing their cries and watching their amazing acrobatic skills – they can

Swifts spend most of their time flying. They can feed, mate and sleep while on the wing.

fly at seventy-five miles per hour – was hypnotic. It was impossible to take photographs because of their speed, but the sight and sound of them will remain with me for a long time.

Swifts are at risk worldwide. Their numbers are diminishing and it is heart-warming to know that there are groups, like those in Israel, who care enough to try to educate others about the need to preserve these tiny miracles of nature.

It was refreshing to visit this sometimes-contentious site for a ceremony that, while neither religious nor political, confirmed Israel's regard for such small creatures and its commitment to their protection.

Thousands of coins from the 4th century BCE to today have been unearthed, as well as fragments of pottery, jewelry and weapons.

The Temple Mount Sifting Project

Family hunting for treasures

Jerusalem is probably the most excavated city in the world. The only part that has never been touched is the Temple Mount, which occupies one-fifth of the Old City. This is because the area has for years been under the control of the Muslim Wakf, which has never permitted digging there.

The Temple Mount is of great significance for Jews, who face in its direction to pray wherever they may be in the world. Here Abraham offered his son Isaac as a sacrifice to God, here Solomon built the First Temple which stood for four hundred years, and the Second Temple was built here and remained from 516 BCE until 70 CE.

This area lay undisturbed until 1999 when the Wakf began illegally building an underground mosque to house ten thousand worshippers. Heavy earth-moving equipment ripped up the ground with no regard to the fact that the soil might contain artefacts of great historical interest. A second underground mosque was then built and four hundred trucks were filled with earth from the excavations and dumped unceremoniously in a waste tip in the Kidron Valley.

Professor Gabriel Barkay, a leading Israeli archaeologist, was convinced that this soil must contain significant findings. In 2000 he applied to the Israeli authorities for permission to examine it and in 2004 the mammoth sifting process began. Mechanical equipment was used in the early days, but the team soon began sorting by hand to avoid damage to anything that might be found. With such a massive amount of earth, it was necessary to recruit volunteers and to date more than one hundred thousand people from all over the world have taken part.

Many unique pieces have been unearthed, the earliest being an arrowhead from 15,000 BCE. Over six thousand coins have been found dating from the fourth century BCE to the present day, as well as thousands of fragments of pottery, weapons and domestic items such as combs and jewelry.

The Wakf claim that both the soil and the finds are from somewhere other than the Temple Mount. There is, however, irrefutable evidence that it definitely comes from there because of the many pieces of glazed tiling and gilded glass mosaic unearthed which at one time covered the Dome of the Rock. The Arabs claim that the Temple Mount is and always has been the province of Muslims alone, even, as they state, since pre-Muslim times. They persist in this somewhat unusual notion despite the mass of finds on the Temple Mount that attest to the presence of Christian, Jewish, Turkish and other peoples going back thousands of years, both before and after the advent of Islam.

It is significant that the prophet Muhammad never came to Jerusalem nor is the city mentioned anywhere in the Koran. In contrast, it is referred to almost 350 times in the Jewish Bible.

To date less than half of the earth has been examined. Dr. Barkay estimates that it could take another fifteen years to complete. It has captured the imagination of archaeologists and historians as well as laymen who simply want to be part of

Volunteers preparing the sieve

something that has great meaning. In a unique way, this project is discovering treasures that significantly add to our knowledge and understanding of days gone by.

It will be exciting to follow its progress and hear about the new finds as they emerge. The work continues. Anyone can volunteer. It provides a rare opportunity to hold in one's hands soil that comes from one of the holiest sites known to man, to experience the thrill of discovery and to feel a direct connection with the past.

Treasure Revealed

Piles of stones at Timna, containing copper

We drove half an hour north of Eilat, pulled off the road onto a dirt track and came to a halt in what appeared to be a wide plain, with hills on either side. There, five hundred yards away, we saw several large mounds of black stones.

Alon, my friend and guide, first discovered this place forty-five years ago when as a young man he was working for the Parks Authority. He himself had fenced off this area with stakes and wire to protect it, and although the barrier was now broken, the land still seemed untouched by either footprints or vehicle tracks. After all, why should anyone want to visit a pile of stones?

Academics and researchers surmise that these

rocks had remained here for between four and six thousand years, from the time when copper mining at Timna had been at its peak. The process of extracting pure copper ore from sand and rock necessitated firing to a great heat. At Timna I had seen how the miners made small fires using foot bellows, but this was evidence of work on a much larger scale.

It is believed that the miners transported the material on donkeys from Timna, six miles away, and constructed huge fires at this very location, in all likelihood using the plentiful wood that could be found a short distance away in Jordan. It seems that this place was chosen because it has a prevailing wind that would have been advantageous for fanning the flames needed to heat up large quantities of metal ore.

Copper was of tremendous importance for those early civilizations. Not only was it used for decorative purposes, jewelry, vessels and so on, but more importantly – it was essential for the manufacture of weapons and tools.

Much the same can be said for copper production today. And it was serendipitous that, while clambering over this hoard, I came across two small metal items glinting on the sandy earth. They were made of copper. Both were casings from bullets – one from 1948, the second from 1958, as proven by the dates stamped on them.

Who manufactured these copper items? Who fired the guns? Why was there conflict in this

While clambering over this hoard, I came across two small metal items glinting on the sandy earth. They were copper casings from bullets.

area and what were the battles about? And so the mysteries continue….

These are the marks of history. Perhaps in another few thousand years someone else will find them and try once more to unravel the mysteries of the past.

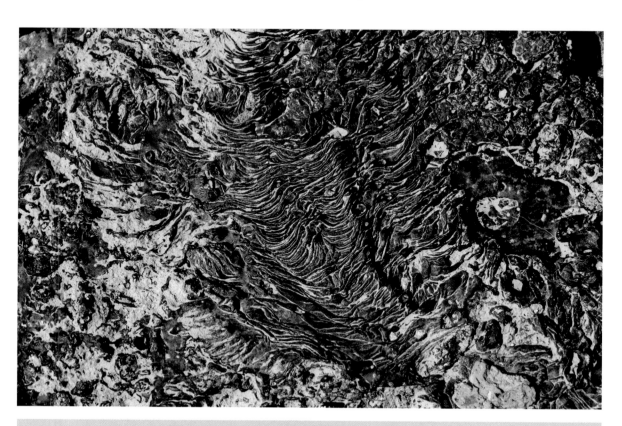

Stone landscape

> "My people
> will abide
> in peaceful
> habitation,
> in secure
> dwellings
> and in quiet
> resting
> places."
> (Isaiah 32:18)

Turning Again

Restoration work on old windmill

One of the more unexpected landmarks seen in Jerusalem is the Montefiore Windmill, at Yemin Moshe.

Built in 1857 by British Jewish philanthropist Sir Moses Montefiore, it was intended to produce grain and thereby provide employment for a few of the impoverished Jews living in squalid, overcrowded conditions in the Old City and to help them become self-sufficient. Montefiore encouraged their move to a new residential area outside the city walls, and to this end in 1860 he built almshouses next to the windmill at Mishkenot Sha'ananim. The name was taken from the Isaiah 32:18: "My people will abide in peaceful habitation, in secure dwellings and in quiet resting places."

The area, however, was subject to raids by brigands and consequently was neither "peaceful" nor "secure." The Jews were reluctant to stay there overnight, returning at dusk to the safety of the Old City.

Despite his good intentions, Montefiore's plans for the mill were not so well founded. Anecdotal reports relate how local millers resented the new mill, considering it the work of the devil. A further story tells how Arabs working on its construction developed a liking for the taste of the lubricating oil and would lick it off the bearings. This led to fears that the mill could burn down through excessive friction. The problem was resolved by placing a leg of pork in the oil, which deterred them from continuing their lickfest.

The mill operated for eighteen years. It broke

down several times but no one in Israel was qualified to fix it. Eventually it closed, probably through competition from newer, more efficient steam-powered mills.

During the 1948 War of Independence, Jewish fighters used the mill as a lookout post, but the British authorities blew up it up in an operation they called "Don Quixote," to prevent this usage. In later years it was restored and served for many years as a small museum displaying one of Montefiore's carriages, until this was destroyed by fire in 1986.

In 2012, one hundred and thirty-seven years after the blades stopped turning, the windmill was given a new lease of life, thanks to the initiative of the Jerusalem Foundation and the generosity of Dutch Christian Friends of Israel. A team of experts from Holland was employed to reconstruct the mill.

I visited it after the renovations were completed and was invited to ascend to the top. After scaling precipitous wooden ladders I reached a circular room where the millstone was installed and working.

Jonathan, who runs the operation, started the sails turning. It was a windy day and truly dramatic to see them whirling past so close to where we stood.

I was curious to know how he came to be working as a miller. He said he had emigrated to Israel from Buenos Aires, but had trouble learning English and so could not finish his academic studies. Instead he turned his hands, literally, to the practical skills of carpentry and metalwork – ideally suited for working in the mill.

Then, quite coincidentally, he met and married a Dutch girl, whose father happened to be one of the leading windmill experts in the Netherlands. Their family home was a windmill. Her brother had been born in it and she had spent most of her early years living there. It was a chance in a million that this girl from such an unusual background should find herself living with the one and only miller in Israel.

Jonathan loves the challenge of bringing history back to life and now makes whole wheat flour for sale to the many visitors who flock to see the windmill turning.

Jewish tradition states "If there is no bread, there is no Torah [Jewish law]," meaning that if you do not have enough to eat, you will not have the energy or resources to study Torah. Sir Moses Montefiore would be delighted to know that his windmill is once again providing an opportunity for someone to earn his "daily bread" and by extension, receive spiritual sustenance from studying Judaism.

The restored windmill

Under Their Very Noses

On a wooded hillside outside Rehovot lies a small museum. Called the Ayalon Institute, it tells a story of outstanding courage, ingenuity and audacity displayed by a group of young, dedicated pioneers.

This dramatic tale begins in 1945 when the Jews, living under the UK Mandate, anticipated the probability of fighting breaking out with the Arabs, if and when the British were to leave.

Leaders of the Haganah (precursor to the Israeli army) were deeply concerned about their ability to defend themselves. They had produced 450 Sten guns, but had hardly any ammunition. Moreover, if Jews were found in possession of weapons, they faced imprisonment or even execution at the hands of the British.

How could they possibly find a way to manufacture desperately needed bullets in such circumstances? Their solution was so outrageous that had you seen it in a movie or read it in a novel you would never have believed it possible. They decided to build what appeared to be a regular kibbutz, but twenty-five feet underneath it they constructed a clandestine bullet factory, the length of a tennis court.

To undertake such an ambitious project, reliable volunteers had to be found who understood the need for absolute secrecy and who could adapt to the rigors of working underground. Many of those selected had arrived as refugees from Germany, Austria and Czechoslovakia after experiencing the horrors of Nazi Europe. They were eager and ready to help their new country in its time of need. Most of them were under twenty.

The kibbutz they built comprised accommodation, a children's house, a dining room, a laundry, a bakery, chickens, gardens and fields for agriculture. To passersby it was a simple farming community, with nothing to indicate what lay beneath.

The factory took three weeks to excavate and cover with earth, and another two to dry out the underground rooms so that a ventilation system could be installed, with air being replaced eight times an hour.

The major concern was access – one entrance was required for workers to come and go and a second for use in emergencies and for lowering machinery. Camouflage was crucial. The first entrance, measuring a mere twenty-two by twenty-six inches, was hidden under a washing machine in the laundry. The second, measuring about seven feet by ten feet, was concealed under the ten-ton base of an oven in the bakery. Electricity and water were supplied courtesy of His Majesty's Government by illegally connecting to the mains.

Work began at 7:00 a.m. daily. The first shift of forty-five workers strolled through the kibbutz carrying farming tools as if heading for the fields. Instead, they entered the laundry. The washing machine was moved aside and, as if by magic, forty-five people disappeared underground in less than ninety seconds.

It is impossible for us to fully appreciate their working conditions. They operated two ten-hour shifts and the noise of hammers and lathes made it impossible to hear or communicate. Some sang while working and others guessed, by lipreading, what they were singing and joined in. Meanwhile the washing machine pounded away upstairs to detract from this noise.

Inquisitive onlookers occasionally asked why the kibbutz washing machine worked nonstop. So

Entrance under washing machine

to increase their official "work load," a shop was opened nearby where locals brought their dirty linen. A maternity home in Rehovot used their services, as did soldiers from the British camp. I watched a film interview with a veteran worker, who recalled that "the British liked us because we did such an excellent job cleaning their uniforms." Customers never collected their washing – it was always delivered to them to avoid their coming to the kibbutz.

British troops, however, carried out routine security checks. On one visit they were offered beer but complained that it was warm, so one bright kibbutznik suggested that if the soldiers notified them in advance of their next visit, beer on ice would await them. The soldiers agreed and

Machine for stamping out bullets

this provided a perfect way of knowing when they would turn up.

Noise, while stressful at work, could sometimes be advantageous. A train carrying British troops passed close by several times a day. As it approached, the clatter from the train provided the perfect soundproofing for the workers testing bullets in the subterranean shooting range. When the train passed, the shooting ceased until the next one came along.

Being underground for long hours caused health issues. The workers lacked fresh air and sunshine and were noticeably pale, unlike the usual nut-brown kibbutzniks. Accordingly, sunray lamps were installed to provide daily treatment and produce "tanned" complexions. Diets were also monitored to ensure the right food and vitamins.

After each shift, clothing had to be carefully inspected to ensure that no fragment of metal remained that could reveal what the workers were actually doing. Unusual wear and tear on shoes caused by metal shavings was noticed by the local shoe repairer, so they opened their own kibbutz shoe-repair shop. Outsiders were discouraged from visiting the kibbutz by notices warning of foot-and-mouth disease – the ruse kept them away.

The group was constantly exposed to danger. Not only was there the possibility of discovery by the British, but working with gunpowder in a closed underground area meant that there was a constant risk of explosions. They had to be scrupulously careful to avoid accidents. Miraculously, during the whole time that the factory operated there was not a single incident.

The institute operated until 1948, and the establishment of the State of Israel. Its contribution to the success of the War of Independence was of major significance: in three years the institute produced fourteen thousand copper bullets a day, totaling over two and a half million bullets. Incidentally, the customs permit to import copper was obtained by telling the British authorities that the copper was used to make lipstick cases, a fact confirmed by gifts of lipsticks to the British officers' wives.

After the War of Independence, the institute's equipment was moved to Tel Aviv and the workers left and settled in Kibbutz Ma'agan Michael. It was only in 1975 that the Ayalon Institute was rediscovered and restored to its original working condition, becoming a National Historical Site in 1987.

I spent two fascinating hours there, seeing the kibbutz and the factory just as they had been when operational. I heard incredible stories about the workforce and was left with an abiding memory and great admiration for those who combined bravery, inventiveness and imagination with a large dose of chutzpah.

What struck me especially was the matter-of-fact way that Shlomo Hillel, who at age twenty-two had been the leader of the group, spoke of his experiences in a televised interview. When asked why he had done what he did, he replied quite simply: "There was a job to be done so we got on with it." If you were to suggest to him that he had been a hero he would have shrugged his shoulders and looked at you in surprise.

I read somewhere that heroes have been described as "ordinary people who do extraordinary things." To my mind, Shlomo Hillel (years later to become speaker of the Knesset) and his fellow bullet makers were heroes by anyone's standards.

The laundry drying on the kibbutz

Vermin Exterminators Inc.

An owl at work catching prey

Pest control is a major concern for farmers in Israel as elsewhere. Today the green lobby discourages the use of chemicals that have a limited effect on rodents but a damaging effect on soil and water systems, ultimately entering the food chain to affect humans.

To resolve this problem, an innovative solution was devised by Prof. Yossi Leshem, an ornithologist. He advocated employing the services of barn owls whose natural instinct is to hunt and kill rodents. With the help of Israel Military Industries, old ammunition cases were requisitioned as nesting boxes and placed in fields two hundred to four hundred yards apart. These soon attracted the owls, which began to nest and begin their work as "vermin exterminators extraordinaires." A perfect example of "beating their swords into plowshares" (Isaiah 2:4).

This system also has side benefits. Israel is located on one of the world's main migratory paths for birds, but for years many were found dead as a result of eating prey poisoned by rodenticides.

Eliminating chemicals and using owls instead has helped to reduce this risk to birds, several of which were becoming endangered species.

Today there are around three thousand nesting boxes in use, located not only in Israel but also in Jordan and the Palestinian Territories.

In Jordan owls were hunted for sport, where tradition held that they brought misfortune. A media campaign was launched there to promote the understanding that far from being harbingers of bad luck, their owls could be harnessed to bring considerable benefits to farmers. Today, conservationists, scientists and farmers from all three areas meet regularly in Israel, exchange information and learn how to manage and extend the project.

Webcams installed in the boxes follow the daily life of the owls. It is recorded that they can produce up to three broods of chicks a year.

Tel Aviv University researchers estimate that one pair of owls can catch between two and five thousand rodents per year. Farmers with date plantations reported that rats used to nest in their dates, causing untold damage, but the use of owls has all but eliminated this, thereby improving crop yields significantly.

Owls hunt only at night, however, so it was necessary to find a way to extend the process during daytime. This was resolved by using kestrels, which hunt during the day and sleep at night. They too were provided with nesting boxes, into which they readily settled. Kestrels and owls are now the perfect partnership, providing a twenty-four-hour organic "ratbuster" service to eradicate pests.

The project partners – Tel Aviv University, the Society for the Protection of Nature in Israel, the Amman Center for Peace and Development and the Palestine Wildlife Society – show how through using birds, which know no boundaries,

A twenty-four-hour organic "ratbuster" service is now in place – barn owls at night and kestrels during the day.

productive and peaceful relations can exist between people of all three countries.

The hope for the future is that this scheme will now extend to neighboring countries so that their farmers too can benefit by achieving the same positive results.

Photo: Hagai Aharon.
Courtesy of Yossi Leshem

A Jordanian farmer holds a barn owl at Kibbutz Sde Eliyahu, Israel, in a joint seminar with Palestinians, Jordanians and Israelis.

Voluntarism

Young volunteers collecting citrus fruit

Helping others in the community is a Jewish tradition going back to biblical times, based on the injunction "Love your neighbor as yourself." Welfare organizations traditionally covered all aspects of life from cradle to grave and were run by volunteers. This continues today. In the religious sector special funds are set up called "*gemach*s," which provide items on loan for needy families such as wedding dresses, pots and pans and so on. Anyone who has something surplus gives it to a *gemach*, where it is redistributed.

Today it is estimated that 20 to 30 percent of all adult Israelis volunteer in one way or another. There are hundreds of registered organizations dealing with First Aid, the handicapped and disabled, the poor and hungry, soldiers' welfare, women's support groups, help for immigrants – just about everything. Charitable work is not confined only to Israel. Teams of volunteers travel worldwide in the wake of international disasters providing rescue assistance of all kinds.

One particular organization that is close to my heart is Leket Israel. Their founders came up with the brilliant idea of collecting food, that would otherwise go to waste, in order to distribute it to the needy. Today they have more than forty thousand volunteers, comprising teams who gather thirteen million pounds of produce from farms and orchards that would otherwise be left to rot. This is delivered free of charge to over 290 non-profit organizations, who in turn pass it on to Israel's needy.

Leket also collect a range of items from food companies that might otherwise go to waste, such as products that are almost at their sell-by date. In addition meals are regularly collected late at night from restaurants, food malls and caterers at wedding halls.

"Sandwiches for Kids," one of Leket's programs, enlists hundreds of volunteers to prepare and distribute over one million sandwiches a year to one hundred schools, from Safed in the north to Netivot in the south of the country. Leket has also set up an advice service about nutrition, as well as a Food Safety Support Program to ensure proper handling, storage and safety of the food they collect.

Twenty to thirty percent of all adult Israelis volunteer.

Collecting food in this way cannot operate in the United Kingdom because of food and safety regulations. One charity does collect tinned or packaged food but it is a much smaller operation, in spite of Britain being a much larger country.

In Israel they have developed a highly sophisticated system, a perfect example of recycling at its best and operated in the main by devoted helpers. Thankfully voluntarism is alive and well and very much a part of the Israeli ethic. It seems that Israelis have taken to heart the old adage: "If I look after myself alone, what kind of a person am I?" (Mishnah *Avot* 1:14).

Courtesy of Leket Israel Archives

Collecting vegetables

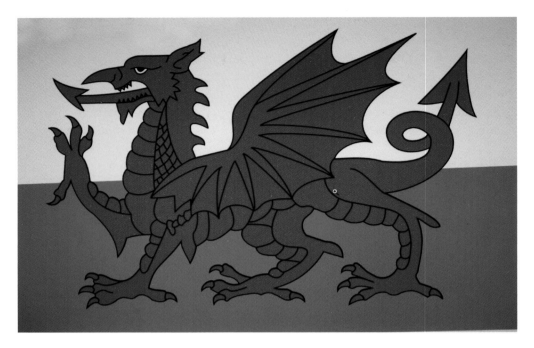

Wales and Israel

In 1988 I helped to arrange a visit to Israel for the Maelgwyn Male Voice Choir from Wales. Twice winners of the Eisteddfod Festival, this two-hundred-strong group of men born into the Welsh musical tradition realized a lifelong dream to visit the "Holy Land." Their trip coincided with Israel's fortieth anniversary and – a lesser-known fact – the four-hundredth anniversary of the translation of the Bible into Welsh.

Much has been written about the connections between the two countries. Geographically the same size, they both have biblically named towns such as Bethel, Nazareth, Carmel, Hebron and Caesarea. So esteemed were these biblical names that it is said that some of the Jewish itinerant peddlers in Wales in the nineteenth century would change their names to Isaac or Jacob as

they thought it would be good for business. In 1917 it was volunteers from some of these Welsh villages who marched with the 53rd Welsh Division to Palestine to liberate the population from Ottoman Rule.

There are those in Wales who believe that they are one of the "lost ten tribes" of Israel. This claim is backed by the fact that both languages use words in common – one example being the Welsh Wlpan and the Hebrew Ulpan, both meaning centers for language teaching. Linguistic experts, however, are skeptical.

In 1926, Kibbutz Ramat David was established. It was named not, as most people assume, after King David of biblical fame, but rather after David Lloyd George, the first Welsh prime minister of Great Britain. Lloyd George was a devout evangelist. In 1925 he told the Jewish Historical Society of England: "I was brought up in a school where I was taught far more history of the Jews than about my own land. I can tell you all the kings of Israel, but I doubt if I can name even half a dozen kings of England" (Stephen Sizer, *Christian Zionism – Roadmap to Armageddon?* [Leicester: Intervarsity, 2004], 63).

It was the Scot Arthur Balfour, another evangelical Christian, who as foreign minister in Lloyd George's government authored the Balfour Declaration of 1917, supporting the establishment of a Jewish homeland in Palestine. The efforts of these two dedicated men helped to lay the foundations for the future State of Israel.

The Maelgwyn tour was eventful, not the least because so many of the men shared the same family name – Jones, Hughes and Evans – in addition to twenty-four choir members called Williams. This created chaos on their arrival at Ben Gurion Airport.

Their tour began in the Galilee and continued to Jerusalem. Here I met them and together we traveled to Rehovot. On the bus the choir asked me to teach them a Hebrew song that they could sing at their last concert. I suggested "Heveinu Shalom Aleichem," which, having only three words, seemed a good choice. Each man wrote them on his hand or arm and we practiced enthusiastically during the journey.

At the end of their performance in Rehovot, I addressed the audience to announce that the choir had a little surprise for them. The men then gave a rousing rendition of "Heveinu Shalom Ale-ichem" in a five-part harmony that raised the roof. There was scarcely a dry eye in the house. A few weeks later the choir accepted my invitation to sing at Israel's fortieth-anniversary celebrations in London. By now they were like our extended family and once again they won over the audience with the power of their magnificent voices. I have shivers when I recall it.

For twenty-five years we were not in touch, until very recently when I called them up they regaled me with their reminiscences, remembering everything about their trip to Israel. My mission is now to visit the "land of their fathers" to share with them memories of their journey to the "land of my fathers." I can't wait!

"I can tell you all the kings of Israel, but I doubt if I can name even half a dozen kings of England." – David Lloyd George

Emptying God's mailbox is not a simple operation.

The Western Wall

Hand on the Wall

The Western Wall in Jerusalem is the only remaining part of the Second Temple destroyed by the Romans in 70 CE. It is one of the most visited tourist sites in Israel. Not only is it a holy place for Jews, but it also has great significance for peoples of other religions.

There is scarcely a time that I go there that I do not see hordes of tourists coming to pay their respects. Many of them are fundamentalist Christians – from all over the world. They approach the Wall slowly and with reverence and after a few moments of contemplation or prayer take their leave, walking backward as a sign of respect, much like we do in England in the presence of our royalty.

This devotion for the Wall and what is represents is manifested in many ways, not the least the custom of writing a note and finding a nook or

cranny in which to place one's words in the hope that God will read them and respond. Approximately one million notes are left each year. These are removed twice annually before the Jewish holidays of Passover and New Year.

Empting God's mailbox, however, is not a simple operation. A team of workers carry this out under the supervision of the rabbi of the Wall, who ensures that the notes remain confidential and are then buried, as many of them will contain the name of God. The rabbi also recites a special prayer, asking God to answer the requests that are contained in the notes.

Last year I had a guest staying with me in Jerusalem. She is a Christian Copt whose father came from Egypt. She decided that she wanted to write something. After breakfast I provided her with notepaper and left her to compose her letter. Forty minutes later she was still writing. She had by then filled two A4 pages in very small, neat handwriting. Eventually she got close to finishing the letter and turned to me for advice.

"Well," she said, "I've completed the letter but I have never written to God before so I don't quite know how to sign off."

"That's obvious," I replied. "It must be 'Yours *faith*fully.'"

Placing a message

The White City: Tel Aviv

Sadovsky house, designed by architect Carl Rubin, 1933

My first link with Bauhaus architecture in Israel was over thirty years ago, when I visited the Weizmann House in Rehovot. I was then director of the British Israel Arts Foundation and the first event I organized was a major exhibition of Israeli architecture in London. It was a learning curve, but I was hooked!

I learned that Tel Aviv was the first city in the world to be built in Bauhaus, or International, Style. International Style was the name used in America, whereas Bauhaus stemmed from the school of that name which existed in Germany from 1919 until 1933 when the Nazis, claiming that it was the center of "communist intellectualism," closed it down.

This led to some twenty Jewish architects, teachers and students of the Bauhaus, fleeing to British Mandate Palestine. The group included luminaries such as Dov Carmi, Ze'ev Rechter, Richard Kauffmann and Erich Mendelsohn, designer of the Weizmann House. Their talent and personalities undoubtedly led to Bauhaus becoming the dominant architectural style in the country, especially in Tel Aviv.

Bauhaus advocated a move away from former architectural styles featuring ornamentation. Instead, the emphasis was on functionality and the use of inexpensive building materials such as concrete. Decorative forms such as cornices and eaves were rejected as "bourgeois frivolities." This approach married well with the socialist ideology prevalent in the land of Israel at the time, as well as the pressing need to provide cheap housing for the thousands of refugees arriving on its shores.

In Tel Aviv a large number of workers' apartment buildings were erected. These blocks included essentials such as a post office, nursery school, laundry and local store. Another underlying principle was that residents should have access to green space, not only for leisure but also for growing plants and vegetables to "link them with the land," another objective of the early settlers.

Bauhaus designs were cubic with clean simple lines, flat roofs, balconies and open-plan interiors. Certain aspects were modified to suit the Middle East climate. Large, conventional windows were abandoned and in their place narrow, horizontal strip windows, similar to those of Le Corbusier, were installed to keep out the hot sun and glaring light. Buildings were constructed on "pilotis" or stilts, leaving the ground floor free, to allow sea breezes to reach as far inland as possible and also to provide a "green" area for residents.

Today there are more than four thousand Bauhaus buildings in Tel Aviv. Many had become run

Another good example of Bauhaus architecture

down, but the recent trend has been to renovate them, largely because of the high cost of land and the increasing demand for apartments. In 2003 the "White City" of Tel Aviv became a UNESCO World Heritage Site, considered "an outstanding example of new town planning and architecture of the early twentieth century."

Tel Aviv has a small Bauhaus museum where a visit can be combined with tours of some of the more interesting buildings. I went on a walking tour of twenty or so of the buildings with a recorded commentary and learned quite a few things that I hadn't known before. I was surprised to see one of the houses with a tiled frontage, as ornamentation was frowned upon by Bauhaus. This was explained by calling it "unfunctional functionality." It seems that many of the refugees from Germany and Austria had to leave quickly without any money. They could, however, take practical things such as furniture, or doors, window frames and in this case tiles, in the hope that these could be used in a practical way once the refugees reached Palestine.

Hampstead in London, where I live, has a fine though small collection of Bauhaus buildings, largely designed by Jewish refugees who came from Central Europe. Some of these were originally planned as homes for industrial workers. However, the high construction costs led to many of them being sold to the very bourgeoisie for whom they were never intended.

In the mid-1930s a Hungarian refugee architect, Erno Goldfinger, moved to Hampstead and built a home for himself in an exclusive area where most of the residents lived in traditional Victorian or Edwardian mansions. They hated Goldfinger's house with a vengeance.

One of the residents was Ian Fleming, the author of the James Bond stories. He was incensed by this "abomination" being constructed near his home. He tried all means possible to have Goldfinger's plans aborted, but he failed and the house was built.

Fleming, however, had his revenge. Twenty years later he wrote a book that became an international best seller about Goldfinger, an arrogant, self-absorbed criminal. The architect Goldfinger took legal action about the use of his name, but the case was settled before trial.

By then, however, the damage had been done, demonstrating the truth in the adage "Revenge is a dish best served cold."

> Tel Aviv is an outstanding example of new town planning and architecture in the early twentieth century.

White Rocks

Cliffs at Rosh Hanikra

Geology was never a subject I was familiar with, but when Alon suggested seeking out special places where pure white rocks were to be found throughout the length of Israel, I agreed, though somewhat skeptically. He explained how three kinds of white rock are found in the country: chalk, dolomite and nari. The last being a hard limestone that is found covering layers of chalk.

We began our travels at Rosh Hanikra on the northern border with Lebanon, where soaring white chalk cliffs hug the shoreline, and spectacular grottos are carved by erosion from the pounding sea.

It was here, at the start of World War 1, that the British decided to build a rail link from Cairo to Beirut and Tripoli in Lebanon. With the support of ANZAC forces, tunnels were bored into the cliffs, supporting walls were built to provide protection from the sea and fifteen bridges were constructed along the track – an ambitious undertaking.

The railway served to carry equipment and manpower but it was also the route along which, in 1944, a number of Jewish refugees from Nazi Europe were allowed into Palestine. They were exchanged for German Templars living in the country, whose sons were serving in the German army.

In March 1948, before the establishment of the

state, Haganah fighters blew up the line, fearing that it might be used to transport hostile troops and weapons from Lebanon, which had declared war on the fledgling nation of Israel, along with the other surrounding Arab countries. This action of the Haganah, completed in one night, resulted in a truly explosive ending to what had been a major engineering feat.

We then traveled further south to the region of the Judean lowlands. Here I was introduced to another surprise of nature at Bet Guvrin National Park, where white rock covers 1,250 acres in an area riddled with underground caverns. These were used as burial caves, storage, hiding places and dovecotes. One section comprises eighty interconnected "bell caves." To form them, openings were excavated through the surface nari. Digging continued downward and outward through the softer chalk, creating caves over sixteen feet in height. A small circular opening in the roof allowed light to penetrate.

Archaeologists are not certain who first began excavating, but signs of habitation from Greek, Roman, Hasmonean, Crusader and Arabic periods are evident from the different tool marks chased into the walls.

These bell caves were probably originally dug as quarries, the white chalk being a valuable material for creating blocks for construction and also used as a powder filler when pulverized. This helped to stabilize structures in the event of earthquakes.

Jews used the caves as refuge from the Romans, and as columbaria for breeding doves that were used as sacrifices in the Temple. They were considered to be the most valued offering one could make. Rows of recesses were carved into the walls that provided nesting places for the doves. The small size of the niches indicates that these doves were specially bred with a much smaller wingspan than today's birds.

During the Talmudic period questions were

Beit Guvrin, Bell Cave

asked such as "if a chick falls from its niche on the Sabbath, is it considered 'work' to lift it up and replace it in the recess?" I hope kindness to animals, another important aspect of Jewish thought, prevailed, and that the rabbis consented to giving a helping hand to the poor creatures!

Our last stop in this "white wonderland" was further south, this time to the border with Egypt and the Nitzana Hillocks. Here I was confronted with a unique panorama the like of which I have never seen. Smooth white hills of brilliant white chalk stretched before us, resembling a lunar landscape. I was told that millions of years ago an ocean must have covered this whole area.

The hills, weathered by sun, wind and occasional rain, result in unusual forms, many representing reclining female figures. These in turn are interspersed with other curious shapes where flint, a much harder stone, resisted the ravages of nature and resulted in the creation of mushroom- and crown-shaped tops on some of the hills.

Few people were there as we wandered around, marveling at the sights before us. These were made even more miraculous at sunset as the dis-appearing sun created long, glowing pink shad-ows – which in dramatic contrast to the darken-ing sky provided an unforgettable photographic experience. It was one of those rare occasions when words are totally inadequate – far better

The disappearing sun created long, glowing pink shadows, providing an unforgettable experience.

to remain absolutely silent and simply commit everything to memory. My skepticism about ge-ology disappeared.

Nitzana Hillocks

Wild Flowers

Wild poppies in the Carmel Forest

The commitment of Jews toward the conservation of nature dates back to the book of Genesis where the special relationship between man and earth is spelled out, affirming man's obligation to both protect and work the land. This policy was fundamental to the ideals of the first pioneers who settled the land of Israel and established the kibbutzim.

Israel's geographic location, being at the juncture of three continents and with three climatic regions, has resulted in it having around three thousand indigenous plant species – almost as many as the state of California, which is fourteen times its size.

In 1953 – only five years after the founding of the State of Israel – the Society for the Protection of Nature in Israel (SPNI) was established. In those days it was not uncommon for Israelis to pick wild flowers, with the result that anemones, cyclamen, irises, tulips and daffodils were facing extinction. The SPNI set about raising national consciousness through educational projects, mainly in schools. The result is that today Israelis no longer pick wild

In 1953 many flowers such as anemones, cyclamen and irises faced extinction.

An ancient olive tree and spring flowers

flowers which grow in profusion, particularly in the springtime.

Advertising executives today still cite this campaign to save wild flowers, with a very limited budget, as the most successful one ever mounted in Israel.

There is no room for complacency, however. The ban on picking flowers did not extend to wild herbs. One resident of a village in the north was caught in 2012 with almost nine hundred pounds of the herb gundelia. Hyssop (za'atar) too is under threat, but thankfully there are local initiatives in some areas to replant wild flowers and to stop spraying with those insecticides that can kill them.

The Israel Nature and Parks Authority (formerly, the Parks Authority) has established reserves over 25 percent of the country – a fact that, on the face of it, seems promising. However, 50 percent of these are used as army firing zones, and the parks that do permit visitors tend to be vastly overrun by tourists, resulting in damage to paths, and spoiled by the garbage that is left behind. The magnificent coral reef at Eilat is dying – caused by pollution from sewage, oil spills, fish farms and tourists.

The oasis of Ein Gedi, near the Dead Sea, has also been under threat. For years it relied on water from a local spring, however some of this was diverted to cater for a water-bottling plant in a nearby kibbutz. This, combined with natural phenomena such as flash floods, caused damage to plant life along the narrow canyon of Ein Gedi.

Thankfully a light has appeared at the end of the tunnel. In March 2012 the SPNA organized a Nature and Heritage Conservation Week. Twenty-two nature reserves and national parks were opened free for the public to raise awareness of "endangered flora." Rangers have worked hard to replant many of the species that grew in Ein Gedi sixty years ago but are now extinct. To date they have reinstated thirteen varieties and are in the second stage of replanting up to one thousand trees and bushes in an effort to repopulate the landscape. A complex operation, it also includes research on how to protect plants against foraging of local animals such as the ibex or the rock hyrax.

It is encouraging to know that the many committed organizations in Israel are working together to try to stem this flow of destruction, are aware of the problems and are taking steps to restore the land to its former state.

Wine

For some reason the entire world of wine has always passed me by. I have never understood the point of it, nor the passion and enthusiasm it engenders among connoisseurs.

This attitude prevailed even during my university years when, rather than joining friends at the pub, I spent time interviewing people for my dissertation on "Problems of Being a Non-Drinker in a Drinking Society."

Recently, however, and uncharacteristically, I attended a lecture on wine in Israel, given by an enthusiastic expert on the subject. Surprisingly, my reaction was "Maybe I've been missing something all these years" – not exactly an epiphany, more a gentle nudge to explore the subject and grant it a proper hearing.

Winemaking has existed in the land of Israel for at least five thousand years. Grape pips were found at a dig in Tel Jericho (3,000 BCE) and Egyptian documents of that same period describe "this wonderful land…with figs and grapes and more wine than water." The spies sent by Moses to report on the land of Israel returned with a bunch of grapes so big that it required two of them to carry it – tangible proof of the land's fruitfulness. The image of the spies bearing grape clusters is well-known in Israel, having been adopted by the Israel Ministry of Tourism, as well as Carmel Wineries.

The earliest archaeological find of a wine press was in the Elah Valley, dating back 3,300 years. The Bible mentions wine frequently and the Talmud refers to ten varieties of grapes, but the first person to plant a vineyard was Noah when he reached land after the flood. This notable achievement was somewhat tarnished when he became the world's first drunkard and behaved badly – the less said about that the better.

Owning vineyards and olive groves was the basis for assessing a family's wealth and status. Wine was produced for both domestic consumption and for export. King Herod reported how twice yearly wine was sent to Egypt. There was also trade with Greece and Mesopotamia and recent archaeological finds reveal that Ashkelon was both an important producer and exporter of wine in the seventh century BCE.

This activity was halted abruptly with the Moslem conquest in the seventh century CE, as Islam prohibits the drinking and production of wine. It enjoyed a brief resurgence during the Crusader period, from 1100 to 1300 CE, but the ban on wine was reintroduced even more stringently during the Ottoman period.

In the mid-nineteenth century the ban was partially lifted, allowing the Shur family to establish four wineries. In 1870 the Teperberg family, leading exporters of methylated spirits, established their wineries, hopefully not confusing their two products. Baron Rothschild gave the industry a boost when he imported French grapes and planted vineyards in Zichron Yaakov and Rishon LeZion – the birthplace of Carmel Winery, now the largest in Israel. Coincidentally three of Israel's prime ministers – David Ben-Gurion, Levi Eshkol and Ehud Olmert – all worked at Carmel in their early years. I am not sure what conclusions, if any, one can draw from this.

Wine making in those early years was predominantly of sweet kosher wine for religious uses, but the last twenty years has seen a dramatic increase in viticulture. Forty-seven boutique wineries have opened and Israeli wines are winning major prizes worldwide. Forget Chiantishire, it is now fashionable to take tours in Israel to the wine-producing regions including the Golan, Rishon LeZion, the Jerusalem hills and even the Negev.

In order to learn more, I visited Bravdo, winery situated close to Latrun. There I met Professor Ben Ami Bravdo, who was a faculty member of the Hebrew University of Jerusalem and is acknowledged as one of the leading international scientists of modern viticulture. From him I learned a new word: *oenology* – the science of wine and wine making – as distinct from the growing and harvesting of grapes, which is referred to as *viticulture*. Today both subjects are studied at university.

Ten years ago he set up the Bravdo winery together with his former student, Professor Shoseyov. They travel the world advising wineries, but it is in Israel where they have translated their knowledge and experience into creating their own high-quality wines.

While at Bravdo I was given some wine to taste. My first sip did not inspire, but after savoring it and getting slowly to the bottom of the glass (I had about half an inch), it began to taste great. When I told the professor he smiled and said happily, "Well, it looks like you are beginning to develop a palate." Something I never expected. I look forward to taking this experiment further at the earliest opportunity.

> The first person to plant a vineyard was Noah when he reached land after the flood.

A World
of Silence

Amnon and Jill Damti

Amnon Damti was born totally deaf to Yemenite parents who immigrated to Israel in 1949. Despite having two other deaf sons, his mother did not immediately identify the problem with Amnon, but when he was five years old she was told she must enroll him in a special school for the deaf. She left him there and it was eight months before he saw her again. Amnon always felt different from other children as he was unable to express himself verbally, but it was at this school – where others, like him, were unable to hear – that he felt he could communicate.

At around the age of ten he saw the Bolshoi Ballet dancing *Spartacus* on television. He was wholly captivated by their brilliant and energetic performance and it was then that he decided he must dance. He doubted he could achieve

his dream because of his deafness, but he never stopped hoping.

Fortune smiled upon him, however, when Moshe Efrati, producer and choreographer, saw Amnon dancing in a folk group, recognized his raw talent and invited him to join a new company called "Demama" (silence). Amnon was fifteen years old. Efrati promised "I will make a dancer out of you," and he kept his word. Amnon began classical ballet lessons and within six months he emerged as a professional dancer.

He was blessed with natural ability and a great sense of rhythm that, combined with a powerful physique, enabled him to excel at the high leaps and pirouettes that were part of the choreography.

Efrati then brought hearing dancers from the Batsheva Ballet Company, combined them with his deaf dancers and formed Kol u'Demamah (Sound and Silence). This was the first and only professional dance group in the world to include deaf dancers. The company acquired an international reputation both for its artistic merit and its contribution to the rehabilitation of hearing impaired.

Such was the expertise of the dancers that audiences could not identify which were deaf and which were not. Amnon became their lead dancer for the next sixteen years, winning an award from Gallaudet University, Washington D.C., for being acknowledged as the World's Best Deaf Dancer.

He explained how he "hears" the music. The "bass" tones resonate through the wooden dance floor and he feels the beat as vibrations from his foot up to his knee. Touch and visual signals are other means of communication between the dancers.

In 1983 he met Jill. From America, she was a gymnast and part of a synchronized swimming team. She swam with dolphins and worked in film and television. They became close friends; she learned sign language. They decided to establish a joint performance called "Two Worlds" and then married.

It was this show that I brought to the United Kingdom in 1993. The reactions of the audiences were unforgettable. On one occasion a small boy, wheelchair bound and with mental problems, leapt out of his chair and moved around while seeing them dance. His teachers were in tears, this being the first time he had ever shown such a response.

Jill and Amnon relate many similar stories. One performance in a high-security prison prompted the question "You have danced before the president at the White House – why do we deserve to have you dance for us?" to which Amnon replied that everyone deserves a chance in life, at which all the prisoners cheered. At another show, for soldiers affected by post-traumatic stress dis-

Amnon & Jill – a program from the British Israel Arts Foundation

order, Amnon was asked to divulge the secret of his eternal optimism, bearing in mind his very difficult childhood. They also perform for Arab audiences, who tend to be amazed that dance can be a career choice for a man.

Jill and Amnon never tire of performing, especially since they always receive such positive feedback. At one school a girl stood up and announced that both her parents were deaf. Previously she would never admit this, but now she saw it as a source of pride. Another child pulled her hair back and revealed a hearing aid, something she had always hidden in the past.

"Two Worlds" has been seen in Germany, France, Belgium, Panama, Paraguay and Russia. In London they performed for BBC TV. They also

Despite being
born deaf,
Amnon hears
the music
through
vibrations
from the floor
that extend
from his foot
up to his knee.

Courtesy of Amnon and Jill Damti

Amnon and Jill

danced before President George W. Bush at the White House.

Amnon teaches modern and classical dance to hearing students and he and Jill give workshops at a special company called Na Lagaat (Please touch), comprising deaf and blind actors. This group is also something totally unique to Israel.

In Israel, 2014 was declared "The Year of The Other." Amnon and Jill participated in this project, performing all over the country with the aim of introducing audiences to those who are "dif-

ferent" so as to encourage understanding, acceptance and respect.

Through "Two Worlds" they bring hope and inspiration to those feeling excluded. They open a door to show that everything is within one's reach and that dreams can be realized with determination and will.

The power of dance can transform lives. Amnon is a living example of how with perseverance, courage and talent one can aim for the stars and achieve the impossible.

> "If you save the life of a single person it is as if you have saved the whole world."

TIMES

MAY 15 1987

"Child saved on flight," The Times article, May 15, 1987, SWNS

A Happy Ending: Rescue in the Skies

On April 20, 1987, I returned on an El Al flight from Tel Aviv to London. It turned out to be one of the most memorable days of my life.

On arrival at Ben Gurion Airport I saw a toddler placed in the aircraft on a stretcher. Her parents hovered around, grey and anxious. The child had a severe liver condition, and her only hope of survival was to travel to England immediately to try to find a liver transplant.

The parents had raised money for the flight but not the £45,000 for the operation. They came in desperation. "We put our faith in God," they said. These Israeli parents, of Moroccan descent, had never been abroad.

Once airborne I spoke to them and offered to try to raise money from the passengers. The response from those traveling was immediate.

Children handed me pocket money. Adults gave cash, wrote promissory notes or gave telephone numbers for me to contact them. After an hour or two I asked the steward if I could speak to the business and first class travelers. He refused as I was an economy passenger; then I remembered that a good friend, the late Cyril Stein, was traveling first class. I sent him a message, he came immediately and, on hearing the story, spun into action.

Cyril was a mover and shaker. He took me to the upper deck. Seeing him operate was an education. "I'm giving £xxxx – how about you?" When passengers replied he said, "That's not enough, you can do better!" whereupon they increased their support.

After three hours 50 percent of the money had

been raised. The crew allowed me to speak on the intercom and I said, "We have raised £25,000 but need more, and in the Talmud it is written that if you save the life of a single person it is as if you have saved the whole world (Mishnah *Sanhedrin* 4:5). Please help us."

I was very emotional – it was impossible not to be. A Canadian who had originally offered $75 upped his donation to $2,000 and by the end of the four and a half hour flight, talking and walking the whole time, I reached the target of £45,000.

On arrival at Heathrow the press were waiting but I slipped off the plane unobtrusively, past the journalists and cameramen, and made my way to the airport branch of Natwest bank, clutching a huge carrier bag filled with money.

"I've just collected this on the plane for a sick child, can you take it and give me one check in exchange?" I asked. "Are you a member of this branch?" they inquired, whereupon I opened the bag, dropped everything onto the counter – twelve different currencies – and said, "No, please just do it!" All credit to them, they did.

Back home all I needed was sleep. Two days later a phone call came from El Al. They had received so many inquiries and asked if I would talk to the press. "Please, Ruth, it's a wonderful story – good for Israel and El Al." I reluctantly agreed. During the following week I gave seventeen TV interviews for stations as far away as South America and Australia. Headlines and articles appeared in newspapers worldwide. Everyone wanted to know the story.

A week later the child hovered between life and death. A liver had not been found. Things reached such a parlous state that I agreed to talk on BBC TV News to appeal for a liver. Just before we went on air a call came to say that a liver had been found, from a man killed in a road crash.

> The child recovered in time to celebrate her fourth birthday, an event the parents never thought they would see.

I also received two calls from potential donors offering their livers, but had to refuse gently, explaining that they couldn't donate them until they were dead so "Much appreciated, but no thanks!"

The operation was a success. The child recovered in time to celebrate her fourth birthday – an event the parents never thought they would see.

I spent a year paying hospital bills and dealing with all the administration. I have a huge folder of press cuttings and letters from the many well-wishers.

I chose not to keep in touch with the family. I did not want their gratitude and preferred that they got on with their lives and put this traumatic event behind them. The girl must now be over thirty years of age, possibly with a child of her own. I sometimes wonder how she is and how life is treating her.

I am asked what prompted me do it. I have no idea except it seemed a good idea at the time. I was glad I was there and the experience confirmed my belief in the innate goodness of people. It left me with an abiding memory of the kindness and generosity of the El Al passengers who together saved the life of a child.